EU and the Balkans

EU and the Balkans: Policies of Integration and Disintegration

Edited by

Leila Simona Talani

Cambridge Scholars Publishing

EU and the Balkans: Policies of Integration and Disintegration, Edited by Leila Simona Talani

This book first published 2008 by

Cambridge Scholars Publishing

12 Back Chapman Street, Newcastle upon Tyne, NE6 2XX, UK

British Library Cataloguing in Publication Data
A catalogue record for this book is available from the British Library

ISBN (10): 1-84718-722-6, ISBN (13): 9781847187222

TABLE OF CONTENTS

LIST OF FIGURES

List of Tables

INTRODUCTION

EU AND THE BALKANS: POLICIES OF INTEGRATION AND DISINTEGRATION

LEILA SIMONA TALANI

Integration and disintegration are the two poles of the economic, political and security discourse in an area, the Balkans and Southern Eastern Europe (SEE), which over the past fifteen years has been the stage of dramatic events. Integration and disintegration are the two dimensions of an identity problem that many feel the area can solve by joining the European Union and diffusing its many conflicts in the peaceful waters of Europeanization. However, quite apart from the obvious point that the accession process cannot be taken for granted in relation to many of the new Balkan countries, integration into the EU can be argued as having been and still being a further catalyst for disintegration.

This book assesses the extent to which the integration of the Balkans into the EU will either foster or discourage the integration of the area itself, as well as the winners and losers under this process. The book addresses the topic in a multidisciplinary way. The contributions are the result of a fruitful co-operation between scholars from the Balkans, the UK and the US.

The book tackles the issue of the relation between the EU and the Balkans in all its controversial and contradictory imensions. From the inside-out, or, how the disruptive forces within the Balkans affect and even jeopardise integration in the EU, chapter 1 analyses the very hot topic of nationalism and the impact of nationalism on the disintegration of the Balkans as well as on EU integration. Leaving aside the various definitions and approaches to nationalism, appearances of nationalism-related phenomena have long been perceived as posing serious difficulties in the Balkans and creating obstacles for the region's development and well-being. The events of the years since the end of the Cold War have only further justified the perception that the region is once again considered 'the Europe's powder keg' on account of the failure to curb nationalism in the Balkans. Hence, it is only natural that in its approach to and interaction with the region, the European Union has had to confront the issue of nationalisms. The conventional understanding is that European integration processes and the EU policy on the Balkans in particular mitigate Balkan nationalisms. The first chapter of the book questions this conclusion and argues that European integration processes and various promises and incentives from the Union have a considerable, and yet ambiguous, impact on Balkan nationalisms.

The disruptive or integrationist potential of intra-Balkan politics is also the subject of the two chapters dealing with Macedonia. In one, the author analyses whether there is a potential danger of an independent Kosovo of provoking an escalation of a new conflict in Macedonia. Since the configuration of factors present in early 2001 and which contributed to the mini war in Macedonia are either non-existent or have since improved, the author concludes that there are strong chances that Macedonia will continue along its European integration path instead. From a more integrationist perspective, the second chapter asks how the public in Macedonia influences the process of the EU integration of the Republic of Macedonia and how the public in the EU influences the process of the EU integration of the Republic of Macedonia.

From the outside-in point of view, or how the EU policy of integration affects the internal policies and politics of the Balkans, the book deals with the EU minority policy and the European monetary integration process. With reference to the former, the aim of the authors of chapter 4 and 5 is to explain and discuss the mechanism for imposing and guaranteeing the operation of the EU minority discourse, as well as its immediate implications for the polities and societies in Southern Eastern Europe (SEE). They also discuss the agents who impose it and the internal and external repercussions of the application of this discourse. It is concluded that the minority discourse has proved to be instrumental, especially in view of the conditional assistance which the EU provides to the SEE countries. The conditionality of assistance is intrinsically related to the very way in which the discourse happened to work – by not only setting performance criteria but also making them compulsory, as well as raising public awareness of the necessity and benefits of these criteria. It is also very important to consider the external and domestic actors involved in imposing the discourse, most importantly those actors who communicate the discourse – the opinion leaders, including NGOs, and the media.

Chapter 5 of the book explores, more in depth, the evolution of the EU's Stabilisation and Association Process (SAP) as its primary approach to post (-violent) conflict management in the Western Balkans, drawing on the apparently tried and tested instrument of conditionality for inducing political and economic stabilisation, transformation and integration into the EU. As part of its investigation of the SAP process, the chapter concentrates on the political aspects of stabilisation within post-conflict societies. First, the EU's emphasis on a regional approach to conflict management is scrutinised in tandem with the bilateral dynamics which have underpinned relations between the EU and the states in that region. Secondly, the EU's approach to minority rights is considered against the background of the desire to foster stabilisation and democratisation in the countries of Former Yugoslavia. In this way the chapter raises the fundamental question of how effective an instrument the SAP is for addressing the particular set of post-conflict transformation problems confronting the Western Balkan region.

As far as the 'Euroisation' of the Balkans is concerned, chapter 6 chooses Bulgaria as a case study and asks who wins and who loses from the prospective entry of the country into the Euro-zone. Bulgarian entry in the EU took place in January 2007. In contrast to what is widely assumed, the country will not adopt the Euro as its new currency immediately because it first has to show that its economy has converged with that of the Euro-zone. Once Bulgaria has achieved economic and budgetary results which prove that its economy has converged, it will join the single currency in accordance with the procedures laid down in the Treaty. The contribution in this book assesses the disruptive impact of the implementation of stricter monetary and fiscal policies on Bulgarian society and the extent to which this can result in a decrease in consensus on the EU integration process.

CHAPTER ONE

BALKAN NATIONALISMS IN THE EUROPEAN INTEGRATION PROCESSES: AMBIGUOUS IMPACTS AND CONTROVERSIAL OUTCOMES

MARIA BAKALOVA

Abstract

Despite the various definitions and approaches to nationalism, appearances of nationalism-related phenomena have long been perceived as posing serious difficulties in the Balkans and as creating obstacles for the region's development and well-being. The events of the years since the end of the Cold War have only further justified the perception that the region is once again considered 'the Europe's powder keg' on account of the failure to curb nationalism in the Balkans. Hence, it is only natural that in its approach to and interaction with the region, the European Union has had to confront the issue of nationalisms. The conventional understanding is that European integration processes and the EU policy on the Balkans in particular mitigate Balkan nationalisms.

This chapter calls this understanding into question and aims to explore the impact of European integration processes and EU policies in the region on Balkan nationalism.

Introduction: Contextualising the Problem

From the times of the disintegration of the Ottoman and Austro-Hungarian empires down to the present day, nationalist phenomena have recurred in the Balkans, moulding the destiny of its peoples and playing a significant role in drawing and redrawing the Balkan political map. The developments on the peninsula following the end of the Cold war drew attention – scholarly and political alike – back to Balkan nationalisms, invigorated images of the Balkans as the Europe's 'powder keg' and reinforced perceptions of Balkan nationalisms as a source or factor of significant conflict potential. Once again, forces of nationalism lay at the core of many accounts and explanations: from the bloody dissolution of Federal Yugoslavia, to failed or stagnated democratisations in various countries of the region, to the views of the Balkans as a troublesome and backward corner of Europe. This overwhelming 'return of nationalism' appeared to be merely the more conspicuous aspect of a process eloquently described by Rogers Brubaker (1996: 2) as the "spectacular reconfiguration of political space along national lines" following the end of the Cold War.

This post-Cold War redrawing of the Balkan political space as a process has run in parallel with two other significant processes:

- internal (regional) profound transformation of the political, economic and social organisation of the various political communities (states); and
- external change of the general geopolitical reorientation of the countries in the region towards new exterior anchors and the increasing attention and involvement of these new exterior factors in the region.

The first of these processes is usually addressed in ontological terms as transition to democracy or democratisation. The second concerns the post-Communist reorientation towards inclusion in the European/Euro-Atlantic structures (addressed in terms of European/Euro-Atlantic integration[1]), as well as these structures' role and activities in the Balkans (including among other things their enlargement in the region through the incorporation of new members). These three processes – redrawing of borders along national lines, democratisation and Euro-Atlantic integration have been largely interconnected and have mutually influenced one another.

---

[1] It should be noted that in the Balkan political and common *parlance* "European integration" or "Euro-Atlantic integration" usually means "accession to" or "inclusion into" the Euro-Atlantic structures, i.e. it is used from the perspective of the parts to be integrated, whilst "enlargement" denotes the same process but from the perspective of the "integrator". Thus, in this particular space-time context the way in which "integration" is used is somewhat different, although it is related to the more general and commonplace understanding of "integration" as a process of intensifying political cooperation in Europe and the development of common political institutions as well as the respective outcome of the process.

Within the network of these interlocking processes, phenomena of nationalism in the post-Cold War Balkans interact and thus both shape and are reshaped by the deep transformational and democratisation processes in the region (Brubaker 1996, Harris 2002). At the same time, the end of the Cold War and the subsequent outburst of often violent conflicts in dangerous proximity to the EU borders served as a catalyst for – on the one hand – the deepening of integration within the Union, leading to the development of a common foreign and security policy. On the other hand, those developments precipitated the increasingly active involvement of the Union in the region – first in the field of conflict resolution and 'getting the region back to normality', but in time expressed also in the articulated notions and political projects for the region in terms also of EU enlargement. From the perspective of the region (and the post-Communist political space in general), this signalled the availability and plausibility of the European alternative. The expectations and next-to-unanimous willingness – expressed by both newly-established and 'old' states – to join the 'European club' (initially somewhat romantically referred to as 'returning to Europe') have made the aspiring accession candidates more open and susceptible to external, and especially EU/European incentives, thus making it possible for the EU to (attempt to) influence various aspects of these counties' internal and foreign policies. In recent years this phenomenon has been increasingly addressed in terms of 'EU conditionality' or 'the EU politics of conditionality' (Kubicek 2003).

It should be mentioned that in this triple grid of interlocking processes – 'nationalismising', or the growing importance of nationalisms, democratisation and European integration – academic and scientific attention has been mostly focused on the relationship between EU integration and democratisation (Dunkerley et al. 2002; Kubicek 2003; Vachudova 2005). Less, but still increasing, attention has been paid to the relationship between nationalism and democratisation (Harris 2002, Snyder 2000, Linz and Stepan 1996). The relationship between nationalisms and European integration processes receives the least attention, which may be due – among other things – to the fact that the official European vocabulary refrains from using the term 'nationalism' in relation to EU enlargement .

1. Answers and Arguments

Against this general background, the present chapter addresses the question of the impact of the European integration processes on Balkan nationalisms[2].

One possible way to answer that question would go along the following lines: over the last decade and a half the EU - through its attractive example of economic and political success and through its external activities - has attempted to promote democracy and provide an anchor for reform leading to democratised institutions and policies. From this follows the seemingly intuitive and conventional understanding that, with respect to nationalism, European enlargement processes, and the EU policy on the Balkans in particular, constrain and mitigate Balkan nationalisms. The assumption underlying this conception is that Balkan nationalisms are factors of significant conflict and destructive potential and threaten both the democratic transformation processes in the region as well as regional and cross-regional stability. As such, they must be tackled and countered presumably by the direct involvement and/or influence in the region of regionally external factors (Dunkerly et al. 2002). The pull of the EU and particularly the (promises of) enlargement as one of the EU's most powerful policy tools provides the EU with the means to address the destructive and confrontational Balkan nationalisms.

Questioning this understanding, this chapter aims to explore the impact of European integration processes and EU policies in the region on Balkan nationalisms. It argues that European integration processes in the

---

[2] The use of "nationalism" in the plural is discussed further in the text. "The Balkans" here refers to the political space of the Balkan Peninsula, i.e. the Balkan states (emerging after the dissolution of Yugoslavia as well as the "old" ones) with the notable exception of Greece and Turkey. Neither of these is a post-Communist country. Moreover, as an EU Member State since early 80s, Greek nationalism was exposed to "Europeanization" earlier on. The post-Cold war developments in the Balkans, however, "Balkanised" and more specifically "Macedonised" Greek nationalism, which, on the one hand, included it in the complex set of interrelating Balkan nationalisms (the Bulgarian-Macedonian-Greek nexus with the sporadic Serb interference). On the other hand, as an "insider" to the EU, Greece has been able to inform and influence European involvement in the region. Turkey on the other side, has for a long time (and much longer than the other Balkan states) aspired to EC/EU accession. Initially the only conditions which the Turkish state was faced with were the fulfillment of the economic criteria. Since the 80s however, with the internationalisation of the Cyprus and Kurdish questions, Turkish nationalisms have been brought to the EC/EU's attention and the EC/EU has begun to make its relations with Turkey also conditional upon them.

region in general, EU specific plans and projects, as well as varying promises and incentives from the Union to the region have an ambiguous impact on Balkan nationalisms, since they subdue and transform some forms and appearances of nationalisms, while at the same time stimulating and determining others. More specifically, the conventional understanding can be questioned along the following lines.

First, the above question cannot be satisfactorily addressed within the narrow conceptual framework provided by the underlying assumption. The normative reference to Balkan nationalisms in negative terms is thriving, so much so that the term 'nationalism' itself has been widely used – in academic and political discourses alike – with heavy negative connotations. In order to study the influence of European integration and EU policies on Balkan nationalisms, one needs to go beyond the normative-negative portrayal of nationalism and conceptualise it more broadly as a heterogeneous set of 'nation'-oriented idioms, practices, and possibilities that are continuously available or 'endemic' in modem cultural and political life (Brubaker 1996). Moreover, this conceptualisation and definitional exercise is necessary also due to the mere fact that in the official EU rhetoric "nationalism" or "Balkan nationalism" rarely (if at all) appears, and yet – so the present argument goes – there is a relationship between Balkan nationalisms and European integration, and it follows from this that the conceptualisation of nationalisms and, more specifically, Balkan nationalisms, can enable us to outline the areas and manners of interaction.

Second, the evaluation of the impact of European integration processes and EU policies on Balkan nationalisms should be distinguished from the question concerning the success and/or effectiveness of purposeful efforts to produce institutional or policy changes in a certain setting. In other words, when it comes to Balkan nationalisms, the success and effectiveness of purposefully exerted leverage on issues pertinent to nationalism/s does not necessarily entail the downplaying of nationalism as suggested by the intuition of the conventional understating.

Third, the question under consideration needs to be placed in a broader context that goes beyond the EU intentions and purposeful involvement in the region, including the process of European enlargement. This is the more general context of the ongoing debate within the EU over the addressing by the 'national' and the 'supranational' arenas of a complex set of normative and political practical questions (such as issues of identity, sources of legitimacy, national sovereignty, citizenship) which have a bearing on nationalism as a political norm and as a political practice.

These considerations inform the logic of the remaining part of the chapter, namely: the conceptualisation of nationalism in general and its placement within a post-Cold War context and in relation to democratisation and European integration processes; and the outlining of the areas of European involvement in the region and analysis of their implications in respect to Balkan nationalisms.

2. Conceptualising Nationalism

It is not new that the subject of nationalism is surrounded by the "stultifying aura of conceptual ambiguity" (Geertz quoted in Brown 2000). For Rogers Brubaker, the problem stems from the fact that nationalism serves as both a 'category of practice' and 'category of analysis' (Brubaker 1996). Though useful and noteworthy, this distinction is not enough to shed light on the conceptual ambiguity. The proposed conceptualisation of nationalism builds upon the David Brown's insight about the different conceptual languages of nationalism which see it as an instinct, an interest and an ideology (Brown 2000). Following Brown, nationalism is conceptualised on three different levels.

First, as a sentiment, nationalism provides a strong instinctive feeling of belonging and loyalty of an individual to a particular group – a nation, which motivates and predetermines the individual's behaviour.[3] In this sense nationalism is often addressed in terms of the awareness, assertion, defence or imposition of a particular – national – identity; whereas psychologically it is rooted in the human need to belong and the ensuing drive for the survival and development of that group.

Secondly, nationalism can be conceptualised as an ideology with the following core propositions: the world is made up of separate organisms – nations; each nation is unique and has its own history and destiny; belonging to a nation is of primary importance to human beings; the nation is the source of all social and political power, and loyalty to nation is stronger and exceeds all other loyalties; nations need to be free and secure, which in practical terms means that each nation must be organised as a sovereign state; by extension – the rights of the nation and its state surpass the rights of all individuals (Snyder 2000:23; Smith 1991:74).

Thirdly, nationalism can also be understood as a political phenomenon expressed in specific political practices, acts and behaviour

[3] It should be noted that this is largely how nationalist thinkers and ideologists perceive and define nationalism. On that basis they also explain, evaluate and prescribe the political behavior of individuals and collectivities.

in defence and promotion of the collective cultural and material interests of individuals who are perceived or who perceive themselves as being united by common nationality and belonging to one nation (Harris 2002; Breuilly 1993). Thus, if nationalism is, above and beyond all else, about politics, and politics is about power, power in the modern world is principally about control of the state. That entails conceptualising nationalism through its political context and its political modes as well as through its operational mode, which partially reflects and partially promotes certain sorts of political action. Nationalism is thus defined and classified in terms of political action. Furthermore, this form of politics makes sense only in terms of the particular political context and objectives of nationalism (Breuilly 1993).

That means that in terms of political behaviour and practice, state nationalism is locked into a (usually limited) number of issues which provide the substance of the respective nationalisms. This is referred to in the discourse of Balkan historiography and social sciences as the 'national question' or 'national issue' which has specific and tangible components as well as a spatial dimension. Given the complex history of the Balkan Peninsula and the heterogeneity of the Balkan population, the classical formulations of Balkan 'national questions' concern:

a) the existing population's politically relevant heterogeneity within the country (internal dimension)
b) and/or a group of (perceived) co-nationals and the territory they inhabit outside the country's territory (external territory) which the state needs to protect/take care of.

The main focal points in the 'national issue' - or the essence of the respective nationalism - are long-term and stable through time. What changes are the adopted political strategies, policies and solutions concerning the 'national question'. The substantive core of nationalism can be questioned and possibly even changed or transformed in times of serious and profound transformations, such as those which the Balkans have been experiencing since the end of the Cold War.

Thus, one reason for using nationalism in the plural is that 'Balkan nationalisms' refer to the nationalisms of the various Balkan nations/nation-states. This is the conventional understanding, according to which the state is the main focus of nationalisms, which thus refers to the state as the main subject of nationalism. From this follows the maxim many states – many nationalisms. In the post Cold War setting however, this understanding has been extended to cover also non-state actors as subjects of nationalism. Consequently, there are various nationalisms within one and the same state - nationalism*s* that co-exist and interact within one and the same political space.[4]

Brubaker's triadic nexus of interacting nationalisms provides a good analytical tool for distinguishing between various Balkan nationalisms according to the subjects/actors concerned and the relevant spatial orientation. Within this nexus there are three interlocking nationalisms: nationalising nationalism, external homeland nationalism, and minority nationalism. The first two are state nationalism – respectively internally and externally oriented, while the third is expressed by a non-state actor. These three nationalisms constantly interact and reinforce one another in a triadic relational nexus (Brubaker 1996), indicating external and internal *loci* of potential nationalism, confrontation, and clashes. Thus, methodologically, the nexus offers one possible way of outlining the relevant areas for exploring the EU involvement in the region with respect to its impact on Balkan nationalisms.

The other more general way of outlining the relevant areas of exploration is suggested by the differentiated approach to nationalism mentioned above: as a motivational feeling, as a prescriptive norm and as politics in the form of specific policies and political actions/behaviour. It is difficult to draw a clear border between these three definitional areas – they clearly inform one another and there are numerous connections between the particular definitions ensuing from one or another understanding.[5] However, this conceptual differentiation makes it possible to specify the areas of exploration of the question under consideration. It is the second and third understanding of nationalisms – as an ideology or set of normative principles and as a set of political practices and actions – which make it possible to address the question under consideration meaningfully.

---

[4] For instance, for Brubaker (1996: 66) nationalism represents a "dynamically changing field of differentiated and competitive positions or stances" adopted by multiple actors from inside and outside the field.

[5] Thus for instance, claims about deeply rooted feelings of belonging and loyalty of individuals to their own nation are logically related and lead to a corresponding way of thinking and explaining the world and the resulting normative views, which, in turn, inform behavior and action that can be directed towards the strengthening or articulation of the feeling of belonging and national identity in a particular form.

3. The impact of European integration on Balkan nationalisms

It follows from the above conceptualisation of nationalism that there are two levels on which the impact of the European integration on the Balkan nationalisms can be explored: normative-ideological and political-practical.

a) Normative level – the promotion and defence of a particular form of democracy (liberal democracy) as built on a specific set of political values and norms de-legitimises certain ideas within nationalism and the specific way in which they are formulated. Namely, the notion that the interest of a particular nation (disregarding the particular definition of nation) must be defended 'at all cost' and 'by all means' becomes subject to serious scrutiny. Thus, through the assertion and promotion of the specific set of liberal-democratic values, the confrontational grip of nationalism is de-legitimised on a normative level. (Here it is important to stress the relevance of the normative implications of the relationship between nationalism and democracy in terms of their mutual (in)compatibility and the consequences for the relationship between nationalism and democratisation).

On this normative level, Balkan nationalisms are also subjected to influences in the more general context of the ongoing debate within the EU on the substance and interaction of 'national' and 'supranational' issues of identity, loyalty and national sovereignty. Here, the impact is greater for states which are closer to integration.

b) Political level – as shown above, on the political level nationalisms can be defined more specifically and in a more nuanced fashion according to a set of criteria; on the most general level this concerns the impact on the political behaviour and political stances of a specific subject (a state, a non-state actor – such as a political party or minority) with regards to the internal or external dimensions of nationalism-related issues.

Here, one can distinguish between a number of forms of EU involvement in the region and their respective impact on Balkan nationalisms:

a) Project, actions and initiatives generally for the Balkans – general and common statements relevant for all Balkan countries /actors; these do not refer to or specifically mention 'nationalism' but speak in terms of democracy, the rule of law, human rights, stability/security, etc.

An example of this was the Badinter commission (1991) which arbitrated between the various parts of the dissolving Yugoslavia and established criteria for the recognition of new states. It sent an ambiguous message, justifying and legitimising the principle of national self-determination and the promotion and defence of 'state seeking' nationalisms, also confronting the new states with the issue of the treatment of their minorities as a way to curb aggressive/violent state nationalism towards new minorities. It also enforced double standards in the implementation of the principle of national self-determination; the latter was not uniformly applied. Indeed, Croatia was recognised despite its treatment of minorities, which in turn boosted Croat nationalising nationalism. In general it encourages state-seeking nationalism (as in the case of Kosovo).

Another instance of a similar dynamic is the Royamont process/initiative (1995) (officially The Process of Stability and Good-Neighbourliness in South-East Europe).

Also, the set-up of the Stability Pact for South Eastern Europe (1999), which aimed to strengthen the countries of SEE ended up reinforcing nationalism, even though it was clearly oriented around conflict-prevention. The stabilisation and association processes, as a framework for the European course on the Balkans and Western Balkans in particular, propose a tailor-made, progressive approach introducing a multi-speed concept and thus adding to nationalist pressures.

Finally, in the Thessaloniki agenda, the Western Balkans are separated as a special category of Balkan states.[6]

b) Mediating in bilateral relations on conflicting issues and acting as an impartial intermediary in treaty negotiations, as in the case of the Romanian-Hungarian treaty in Transylvania in 1995 and the Bulgarian-Macedonian declaration of 1998

c) Conditioning the accessions. Conditionality is generally seen in the literature as a policy tool, with some even speaking about the 'myth' of conditionality (Vachudiva 2005, Hughes et al. 2004). Indeed, accession conditions – such as the Copenhagen criteria, are normally framed in general terms, and are common to and applied to all candidates. The monitoring of their fulfilment and implementation, however, is country-specific, which also means taking into account the respective country's nationalism issues. (e.g. Croatia – in all Commission reports there was a very strong emphasis on the country's minority politics and on the relations with neighbouring countries; on the other hand in Macedonia attention is directed at the relations between the two major communities

---

[6] For more information see European Commission, . http://ec.europa.eu/enlargement/enlargement_process/accession_process/how_does_a_country_join_the_eu/sap/thessaloniki_agenda_en.htm as accessed on 21 March 2008

and the implementation of the 2001 EU-brokered Ohrid agreement of 2001[7])

4. Conditionality and Minority Issues

As far as the pertinence to nationalism is concerned, minority issues, (see, for example, the first Copenhagen criterion: 'respect for and protection of minorities'), concern the internal dimensions and interactions of state-minority nationalism; ideally this emphasis on the respect for minorities in accession criteria reduces or curbs state nationalism in relation to the treatment of minorities. As such, EU conditionality on minority issues is generally discussed as an EU 'success' story.

The leverage of the first Copenhagen criterion is said to have diminished with the start of the negotiations (Hughes et al. 2004). However, sensitive issues such as the treatment of minorities continue to figure prominently in the Commission progress reports, even after the start of negotiations (see above for Croatia and Macedonia).

The treatment of minorities is not codified within the EU – there is no *acquis*, and no EU competences (apart from external relations); these are specific requirements for the new candidates only and their introduction is allegedly induced by instances of extremist and confrontational versions of nationalism throughout the post-communist space.

The introduction of criteria for the treatment of minorities aims to neutralise or minimise the negative forms and appearances of state nationalism in relation to minorities. Insofar as this is imposed as a condition by the external environment and is implemented as a result of pressure, the internal conditions are not always and in all places favourable to this. Political elites experience the dual pressure of concomitant EU integration processes together with the imperatives of nation-building and national self-assertion (especially the new states).

The consequence of successfully applied pressure from the EU with regards to minority treatment entails a restriction of nationalism as a state policy at the official/state level. However, as far as public opinion is concerned, nationalism can still thrive or even be fuelled by externally imposed restrictions on the state nationalism – this form of nationalism is a reaction against the imposition from outside of solutions and recipes for the treatment of minorities.

---

[7] For more information see European Commission, http://www.europa-eu-un.org/articles/en/article_6754_en.htm as accessed on March 21, 2008

On the other hand, conditionality on the treatment of minorities legitimises the idea of minority rights and minority claims in principle; it can lead to increased articulation of the demands made by minority leaders (expanding and escalating claims – a good illustration of which is the behaviour of the Albanian community in Macedonia). Under specific circumstances the decrease of state nationalism can lead to the flourishing of minority nationalism (including nationalism characterised by irredentist and separatist claims), which can and often is perceived as a threat by the 'core nation' which expects its state to protect it. Hence, promoting minority nationalism provokes fear and uncertainty which in turn feeds the 'core nation's' nationalism (triadic nexus of Brubaker of interacting nationalisms which leads to ambiguous outcomes)

In the new Member States, nationalism appears in the form of Euro-scepticism and questions the price of the integration project. In this context there is a re-assertion of national identity and the national interest, defined as the interest of 'our' national group against the other national groups in the Union

Moreover, the national-supranational debate within the EU, reifies nationalism and makes it highly relevant. Hence, in the European Union, Balkan nationalisms need not disappear but have to be reformulated

Conclusion

To date, the EU had focused on the inter-state dimension of nationalism: crisis management, conflict prevention, security initiatives, and the imposition of sanctions.

However, in the case of the Balkans, for the first time the EU directly interfered in shaping Balkan nationalisms in their internal political appearance.

Nevertheless, the role and significance of the EU in transforming Balkan nationalisms should not be overstated and should be regarded at most as an intervening variable.

Indeed Balkan nationalisms are not, in the opinion of the author, any special or different form other nationalisms

References

Breuilly, J., (1993) [1982], *Nationalism and the State*, The University of Chicago Press

Brown, D., (2000), *Contemporary Nationalism: Civic, Ethnocultural, and Multicultural Politics*, Routledge

Brubaker, R., (1996), *Nationalism Reframed. Nationhood and the National Question in the New Europe*, Cambridge and New York: Cambridge University Press.

Brunner, G., (1996), *Nationality Problems and Minority Conflicts in Eastern Europe*, Updated and completely revised edition. Gutersloh: Bertelsmann Foundation Publishers

Dunkerley, D., Hodgson, L., Konopacki, S., Spybey, T., and Thompson, A., (2002), *Changing Europe: Identities, Nations and Citizens*, Routledge

Harris, E., (2002), *Nationalism and Democratization: Politics of Slovakia and Slovenia*, Ashgate

Hughes, J., Sasse, G., Gordon, C., (2004), *The Myth of Conditionality. Europeanization and Regionalization in the EU's Enlargement to CEE*, Palgrave

Kubicek, P.J., (ed.), (2003), *The European Union and Democratization*, Routledge

Latawski, P., (1995), "The Problem of Definition: Nationalism, Nation and nation-State in East Central Europe", in *Contemporary Nationalism in East Central Europe*, Paul Latawiski (ed.), Macmillan Press, 1995, pp. 1-11

Linz, J.J., and Stepan, A., (1996), *Problems of Democratic Transition and Consolidation: Eastern Europe, South America and Post-Communist Europe*, Baltimore and London: The John Hopkins University Press

Smith, A., (1991), *National Identity,* London: Penguin Books, 1991

Snyder, J., (2000), *From Voting to Violence. Democratization and Nationalist Conflict*, London: W. W. Norton & Company, Inc.

Vachudova, M., (2005), *Europe Undivided. Democracy, Leverage and Integration after Communism*, Oxford University Press

CHAPTER TWO

THE IMPLICATIONS FOR MACEDONIA OF THE INDEPENDENCE OF KOSOVO—A REPEAT OF THE 2001 CONFLICT?

ZHIDAS DASKALOVSKI[1]

Abstract

Macedonia should not worry about Kosovo being independent. This chapter offers an overview of the current state of affairs in the northern neighbour, especially in relation to Serbia. It considers whether there is a potential danger of an independent Kosovo and an escalation of a new conflict in Macedonia. Presenting the factors that impeded democratic consolidation, it is argued that since the configuration of factors existing in early 2001 and which contributed to the mini war in Macedonia are either non-existent or have since improved, there is a strong chance that Macedonia will continue on its European integration path instead. Macedonia should be concerned if the situation in Kosovo deteriorates to the point where the territory is partitioned.

Introduction

The president of Kosovo, Ibrahim Rugova, died of lung cancer on 21 January 2006 at the age 61. He will be remembered as a historic figure who played a significant role in the events of the 1990's in the Balkans. He did not live to see the results of his life project - the birth of an independent Kosovo. Yet for many the results of the complicated negotiations involving Kosovar and Serbian statesmen and politicians,

[1] Senior analyst at the Center for Research and Policy Making, www.crpm.org.mk.

with the support of the Contact Group, could result in various dangerous scenarios. There are concerns that an independent Kosovo would affect the state of affairs in Bosnia and Herzegovina and Macedonia.

The potential effects of Kosovo's independence on Macedonian security are analysed here. First, this chapter briefly sets out the positions of the two sides and the international community in the course of the negotiations leading up to the unilateral declaration of independence by Kosovo on 17 February 2008[2]. It then goes on to discuss the possible scenarios of Kosovo's new status. It furthermore presents a detailed overview of the Macedonian quest for inter-ethnic stability and democratic consolidation, briefly explaining the causes of the 2001 conflict before analysing the possible implications for Macedonia of the independence of Kosovo.

---

[2] This was the second declaration of independence by Kosovo's Albanian-dominated political institutions, the first having been proclaimed on 7 September 1990. Unlike the 1990 Kosovo declaration of independence, which only Albania recognised, Kosovo's second declaration of independence has already been recognised as of 18 March 2008 by 29 foreign states, including Afghanistan, Australia, Austria, Belgium, Canada, Costa Rica, Denmark, France, Germany, Japan, Peru, Poland, Senegal, Switzerland, Turkey, the United Kingdom, and the United States, with 3 more acts of recognition pending from Croatia, Lithuania and Norway.
However 25 other countries, including Algeria, Argentina, Azerbaijan, Belarus, Bolivia, Bosnia and Herzegovina, Brazil, Cuba, Cyprus, Georgia, Kazakhstan, Kyrgyzstan, Laos, Libya, Moldova, Romania, Russia, Serbia, Slovakia, Spain, Sri Lanka, Tajikistan, Uruguay, Venezuela and Vietnam have officially and explicitly denied recognition, with several more, such as Chile, China, Egypt, Greece, India, Kuwait, Mali, Mexico, New Zealand, Philippines, Portugal, South Africa, Sudan, and Ukraine expressing concern or urging more negotiations. Serbia has stated that it will withdraw its ambassador from all states that recognise Kosovo, and indeed has done so. See
http://en.wikipedia.org/wiki/2008_Kosovo_declaration_of_independence as viewed on 21 March 2008
For more information see International Herald Tribune, 18 February 2008, http://www.iht.com/articles/2008/02/18/europe/diplo.php as accessed on March 21, 2008.

1. Different Agendas and Interests

The official Serbian position regarding Kosovo was that this province could achieve "more than autonomy but less than independence."[3] Serbia's main argument in the negotiations was that 'secession is not tolerated by international law', arguing that it would not forfeit 15% of its national territory, and far less the province that the Serbs view as the cradle of their nation. The advisor to the premier Koshtunica, Aleksandar Simic, for example said that "the status of Kosovo is mainly a legal issue."[4] It was however, difficult to believe that Serbia's chances for success in the negotiation would be high if this was to be its only argument.

Kosovar officials on the other hand asked without exception for independence. The great powers, including Great Britain, France, Germany, and the USA believed that Kosovo should obtain independence. Indeed, confronted by Kosovo's declaration of independence on 17 February 2008, Britain, France, Italy and Germany all confirmed that they would grant recognition, and also did the United States.[5]

Many analysts argue that Kosovo's achievement of independent status was in a way a deserved punishment for Serbia for the crimes of Milosevic's regime over the last fifteen years. The Western powers and the USA in particular maintain that the conflict in Kosovo and all other inter-ethnic conflicts should in principle be solved on the basis of their particular characteristics. The independence of Kosovo should not be a precedent for the resolution of other, future problems. Using Kosovo's independence as an argument for recognising the secession or independence of territories or provinces such as Southern Ossetia would not be possible.[6] Yet it is clear that Kosovo's independence will be a legal precedent which could complicate internal relations in many countries

---

[3] On the Serbian proposal see "Jednodecenijsko zakašnjenje," *Danas* 10th June, 2006.

[4] See in *Нова Српска Политичка Мисао* [New Serbian Political Thought] article by Mario Brudar „Kosovo i Metohija između htenja, realnosti i želja„ at http://www.nspm.org.yu/koment%202006/2006_brudar_kosovo22.htm.

[5] However, a divided European Union agreed to differ over the legitimacy of Europe's newest nation. After several hours of tortuous negotiation, EU foreign ministers averted open conflict over the principle established by Kosovo's independence, issuing a statement noting that the decision on formal recognition lay with national capitals.

[6] See Bruce Jackson, „Međunarodni faktori već odlučili da Kosovo ove godine dobije neki vid suvereniteta„ in *Нова Српска Политичка Мисао*, [New Serbian Political Thought], http://www.nspm.org.yu/Debate/2006_KOS_dzekson.htm

with minority problems. The reservations of EU Member States such as Slovakia, Spain, Romania or Cyprus on whether to accept Kosovo's independence are not unrelated to domestic considerations.

The attitude of Russia is diametrically opposed to that of the main Western powers. Russia sides with Belgrade, claiming that any new status of Kosovo should have been subject to agreement between the Kosovar and Serbian sides. On a number of occasions President Putin drew a comparision between the problem of Kosovo and the unsolved status of Ossetia, Southern Abkhazia and Transnistria regions in Moldova and Georgia which could demand independence if Prishtina were to be successful. Russia had warned that the solution for Kosovo had to be based on general principles and that it would have universal implications, including for latent conflicts in the former Soviet Union. Kosovo could not be treated as a case apart. In fact, for Russia it is important for the issue of Kosovo's status to be solved, not only on account of the situation in the above territories which are under its influence but also out of the fear of extremism in the Caucasus. Russia’s main concerns are that Kosovo’s independence would influence further separatism in Chechnya and other bordering republics currently controlled by Moscow.

China is one of those countries which have or could have serious issues concerning its own minorities, especially regarding its huge Muslim and Turkic population. In addition, the independence of Kosovo could influence Beijing’s relations with Taiwan. It is likely that Kosovo’s independence would complicate even further the situation in Iraq, especially as regards the aspirations of its Kurdish population for an independent state. The solution of the Cypriot question could also be complicated. It is not at all clear whether Western support for Kosovo’s independence would bring to the surface more problems than the democratic world wishes to tackle in the future.

2. Possible Scenarios

Since both parties to the negotiations did not make and were not ready to make significant compromises, it was most likely that the process would result in a forced or imposed solution to the issue, as it in fact did. The international community has, *de facto*, forced Serbia to accept an independent Kosovo. The great powers always denied a division of Kosovo into a Serbian and an Albanian part as a viable option. A partition could hardly be accepted by Prishtina or nationalist elements in Belgrade such as the Radical Party. Only an armed international presence would have, in such a case, prevented a new war breaking out. A division of

Kosovo would also have had regional implications especially regarding the possible radicalisation of the *Republika Srpska*, directly influencing the future of Bosnia and Herzegovina. Radical fractions of the Albanians from Southern Serbia, Macedonia or Montenegro, could also have made troubles.

Although the northern part of the province, Mitrovica and the territory north of the Ibar river, is at the moment majority Serbian and is *de facto* not under the control of the Kosovar institutions, it was difficult to see a partition which would result in this part being awarded to Serbia. In this scenario, not only would most of the Serbs in Kosovo have remained outside Serbia, but they would also be placed in a very difficult situation.[7] If Kosovo were to be divided, the frustrations of the radical Kosovar Albanians would have come to surface and the danger of ethnic cleansing of the remaining Serbs in the province would have dramatically increased.

The plan of the Kosovar Albanians was to avoid a *de facto* partition of Kosovo, though tolerating a number of cultural and other non-essential rights of the Serbian minority. On the other hand, the Serbian negotiating position was to agree on a strong decentralisation process that would benefit the Northern part of Kosovo as well as Serbian enclaves further to the South, such as Grachanica and Shtrpce. For Serbia fiscal decentralisation in Kosovo should have been undertaken in parallel with the redrawing of municipality borders or regionalisation/'cantonisation'. The aim was also to preserve as far as possible the property of the Serbian Orthodox Church in the province. A prevention of events such as those of March 2004, when Albanian extremists burned and destroyed private property and many churches and monasteries around Kosovo was also a priority on the Serbian side.[8]

---

[7] For the Serbs living in Kosovo and their territorial distribution see the report of the *European Stability Initiative*, The Lausanne Principle: Multiethnicity, Territory And The Future Of Kosovo's Serbs, 7th June, 2004. The Serbs that still remain in Kosovo, are estimated at some 100,000, living in small enclaves scattered across the province and to the North of Ibar river, sharing a border with the rest of Serbia. An estimated 200,000 are refugees in Serbia.

[8] Unfounded allegations of Serbs drowning Albanian children sparked fighting in Mitrovica, leading to two days of Kosovo-wide riots that killed 19 and wounded 900. More than 50,000 Albanians participated in anti-Serb riots in a two-day rampage that killed 19 people, injured 900, forced 4,000 persons to flee their homes, and left the UN mission in turmoil. The KFOR and UNMIK responses were disorganised and harmed their credibility, particularly amongst Serbs. See for example, "Collapse in Kosovo", *Europe Report* N°155, 22nd April 2004.

The dangers of a partition seem to have been avoided by the hasty and unilateral declaration of independence of Kosovo of February 2008. Nonetheless, ethnic violence and riots remain a possibility. Although much better prepared than in 2004, it is hardly likely that NATO or KFOR would be in a position to control street disturbances throughout Kosovo.[9] Similarly, it is not clear how NATO would react in the event of turbulence in the Northern part of Kosovo if a solution is imposed that is not in the interests of the local Serbs. In addition, it is unclear how far the negative conclusion of negotiations would lead to Serbia's radicalisation. Are incursions of legitimate Serbian armed forces into Northern Kosovo a real possibility? During the negotiations, statements by the Serbian premier and the leader of the Radical Party Tomislav Nikolic that if Kosovo achieved independence Serbia would declare the province an "occupied territory" did not raise hopes for a peaceful resolution of the issue.[10] However, the main motivation for Serbia to accept independent Kosovo was, and still is, integration into the European Union. At the moment there are no real prospects of receiving this carrot within a short period of time and the leverage of the European Union on Belgrade's politics is minimal. One should also consider the enlargement-sceptical mood in relation to the European Union as a negative factor in this equation. Few in Serbia dared to forecast that the results of the negotiations over the status of Kosovo would have resulted in its independence. When the former minister of foreign affairs of Serbia Goran Svilanovic did exactly that, he was accused by a part of the media as being a traitor.[11] For Serbia and Serb politicians, the destiny of their land was closely related to the fate of Kosovo. The status of the province was a psychological burden for policy makers in Belgrade.

The fact that Agim Cheku was the Premier of Kosovo also complicated relations between Belgrade and Prishtina. Mr. Cheku, enjoyed a very bad reputation in Belgrade. In Serbia he has been charged for war

---

[9] On March 18, 2008 French Nato troops fired warnings shots, hours after a Ukrainian policeman died from wounds suffered in clashes with Kosovo Serbs in Mitrovica. See "UN Officer dies after Kosovo riot", http://news.bbc.co.uk/2/hi/europe/7300015.stm as accessed on March 21, 2008

[10] For a critique of this view see Zagorka Golubovic „Povodom izjave Tomislava Nikolića o proglašavanju okupacije Kosova-Opasan ratni poklič„ *Данас [Danas]* 15th February, 2006.

[11] See in „A milestone on Kosovo's road to independence„ Feb 20th 2006, *The Economist.*

crimes against Kosovar civilians.[12] Cheku was a former commander of a KLA (Kosovo Liberation Army) unit engaged in fighting during the war in 1999, and a leader of the Kosovo Protection Corps. He was a strong leader nominated as premier by Fatmir Sejdiu, the heir to President Ibrahim Rugova. Within Kosovo, Cheku enjoyed strong popularity, one survey identifying him as the most respected politician.[13] The situation did not improve when Hashim Thaci, former chief of the Albanian guerilla forces, was nominated premier of Kosovo on 9 January 9 2008. His first act was to declare the independence of the region "within a few weeks".

3. Macedonia's Ethnic Politics and the Status of Kosovo

What are the implications for Macedonia of the independent status of Kosovo? Amongst Eastern European countries, Macedonia has followed a distinct yet successful transition from authoritarian rule to democracy. Unlike most of the former Communist countries, Macedonia, together with Slovenia and arguably Lithuania, experienced an evolutionary path to democratic rule (Kis 1998:323; Daskalovski 1999). Yet, the peaceful and benign transformation of Macedonian society was preceded by an uneasy period of democratic consolidation. Among the different factors that negatively influenced this process were: the struggle for the international recognition of the country, the Greek diplomatic and economic pressure for the republic to change its name, the disruption of the economy due to the UN sanctions on Macedonia's main trade partner Serbia, as well as the financial impediments resulting from the NATO bombing of Yugoslavia and the Kosovo refugee crisis. None of these factors is however as important for the consolidation of the democratic system as the challenge to the character of the state by Macedonian Albanians.

Macedonia is, without any doubt, a multi-ethnic country. Besides Macedonians, the largest group in the country comprising 64%, of the total population, there are also 25% Albanians, 3% Turks, and 2% respectively Roma, Serbs, and others. The vast majority of Macedonians are Macedonian-speaking and Orthodox, as are the Macedonian Vlachs and

---

[12] Serbia's government spokesperson stated that the "Serbian government holds that is absolutely unacceptable that a person that has to be tried for war crimes is elected to perform any political function." See in „Kosovo Ditches Its Prime Minister„ Zhana Limani, *Balkan Insight*, 3rd March, 2006.
http://www.birn.eu.com/insight_23_2_mac.php

[13] See the results of the survey of Kumt Consulting published in "Agim Čeku i Fatmir Sejdiju na vrhu," *Danas* 10th June, 2006.

Serbs. On the other hand, most of ethnic Albanians, Roma, and Turks are Muslims. While Macedonians populate the whole country, ethnic Albanians are predominantly concentrated in the Northwestern corner of Macedonia, along the border with Albania. Macedonian Albanians also reside in the capital city of Skopje and the towns of Northern Macedonia along the border with Kosovo. In addition to Skopje, Macedonian Serbs also populate the region around the town of Kumanovo. The other ethnic groups are dispersed throughout Macedonia. Given the diverse character of its population and especially the relatively substantial size of the largest national minority, the accomplishment of democratic consolidation in Macedonia was always going to be a difficult task.

Relations between Macedonians and ethnic Albanians have remained tense since the country's independence. Much of the tension resulted from the different perceptions among the two communities of the underlying concept of the Macedonian state. In the early 1990's, both Macedonians and Macedonian Albanians harboured ambiguous feelings towards the disintegration of former Yugoslavia. Macedonians were pleased at having secured independent statehood. On the other hand, they realised that the Macedonian state would face many obstacles from its more powerful neighbours. Since throughout history Macedonia's neighbours have either consistently chosen to deny the existence of a Macedonian people, and hence its right to possess its own state, thus claiming Macedonia and the Macedonians as their own, membership of Tito's Yugoslavia provided Macedonians with a 'sense of security, a sense of security both against unfriendly, even antagonistic states-Bulgaria, Greece, and to a certain extent Albania and against a condescending and patronizing partner and neighbour inside Yugoslavia, namely Serbia' (Rossos 2002:104).

Similarly, for the Macedonian Albanians independence from Yugoslavia was both a blessing and a curse. On the one hand, with the dissolution of federal Yugoslavia and the proclamation of Macedonian independence Albanians from Macedonia escaped the destiny of their Kosovar kindred who suffered under the strict rule of Slobodan Milosevic. Within the fledgling political system of the Macedonian Republic they were to a certain extent able to influence domestic politics. At least in theory Macedonian Albanians were guaranteed all civil, political and social rights. On the other hand, however, Macedonian Albanians regarded the independence of the country and the new frontiers vis-à-vis Serbia as an unnatural and burdensome obstacle to their relations with Kosovo Albanians. Ethnic Albanians in Macedonia perceive Kosovar Albanians as of sharing the same identity (De Rapper 1998). In fact, during Tito's times Prishtina was a regional centre for all Albanians in the former Yugoslavia including those from Macedonia. Prishtina University educated many of the political and social elites of the Macedonian Albanians. For example, Arben Xhaferi, the leader of DPA was educated in Prishtina and for some 15 years he was a director of the province's television station.

Although separated from their Kosovar kindred, Macedonian Albanians feel that they are not a minority in the country. On the contrary they see themselves as equal partners to Macedonians, and have ever since the late 1980's been asking for the corresponding legal status. When in 1989 a new constitution was adopted defining the Socialist Republic of Macedonia as 'the national state of the Macedonian nation' rather than 'the state of the Macedonian people and the Albanian and the Turkish minorities' as previously, Macedonian Albanians vehemently protested. When a similar formula was accepted in the Preamble to the 1991 Constitution Albanian political elites again protested against these developments and demanded that the Albanian community living in Macedonia be given a partner-nation status.

Moreover, 'the demographic superiority of the Albanians over the other ethnic minorities living in Macedonia is the main argument in their struggle to improve the status of the Albanian community' (Babuna 2000:83). Besides, ethnic Albanians represent a significant percentage of the population in the areas which they inhabit in Macedonia, constituting an absolute majority in many municipalities in the Northwestern and Western parts of the country. Moreover, many Macedonian Albanians are claimed to be without citizenship although they have been living in the country for years if not decades, while also a number of ethnic Albanians from Macedonia have emigrated to Western Europe but maintain close contact with their places of origin. Treated as a 'mere minority ethnic group' Macedonian Albanians perceived the new state and its institutions as lacking legitimacy.

On the other hand, throughout the post-independence period Macedonians felt themselves to be endangered and believed that granting partner-nation status to the Albanians would lead to a Bosnia-type situation. Before the Ohrid Framework Agreement Macedonians largely regarded the Republic of Macedonia as their nation-state, in which other ethnic groups enjoyed equal citizenship rights. Macedonian political elites often argued that the minority rights for the ethnic Albanians in the country were on a par with the highest standards of international legislation. Of especial concern to them was the fact that the percentage of the Albanian population in the country has significantly increased in the last decades. Before the conflict in 2001 Macedonians often pointed out that as a result of the very high birth rate of Macedonian Albanians and the migration of ethnic Albanians from Kosovo during the period from 1953 to 1993, the number of the Albanians had risen by 288,670 or 189.2% so that in 1994, the percentage of the Albanians was 22.6% of the total population in Macedonia, compared to 1953 when this percentage was only 11.7.

Their country having been partitioned during the Balkan Wars of 1912-13, Macedonians were faced with harsh assimilative practices, most of which remain in place even today in Greece and Bulgaria. As a result of the long-lasting repression, Macedonians in these countries have been assimilated in great numbers. Macedonians in the Republic of Macedonia have thus felt doubly threatened; not only is their presence in the historic region of Macedonia rapidly dwindling but also, now that there is a free Macedonian state, ethnic Albanians have vowed to take it over both demographically and politically. By and large, rather than expecting sustainable peace or coexistence, 'Macedonians remain mistrustful of the Albanians' true intentions… at worst they suspect designs for a "greater Albania" (or, more commonly, "greater Kosovo")' (Fraenkel 2003:403).

Indeed, the foundations of the new state in 1991 were not fully supported by the Macedonian Albanians. The turnout in the independence referendum was for example 72% and it is most likely that ethnic Albanians did not participate in it, having been persuaded by their partisan leaders. Paradoxically, Macedonian Albanian politicians were generally speaking happy with the changes in the system and took an active part in shaping it. Ethnic Albanian legal experts were involved in the drafting of the new Macedonian constitution. Three ministers of the short-lived (March 1991- June 1992) non-partisan, 'cabinet of experts' were chosen among the ranks of this minority. The 1992 coalition government led by Branko Crvenkovski's Social Democratic Alliance (SDSM), as well as all subsequent cabinets, included one ethnic Albanian party with five ministerial posts. Over the years Macedonian Albanians have occupied an increasing number of posts in the diplomatic service, public administration, the police and the army. Nonetheless, ethnic Albanian politicians in Macedonia 'in the early years of transition, adopted an obstructionist tactic' (Hislope 2003:139).

Thus, the new constitution did not pass an important internal test as it was not approved of by the political parties of Macedonian Albanians. The special parliamentary session was boycotted by the PDP-NDP (Party for Democratic Prosperity – National Democratic Party) in protest against the preamble to the constitution which formally declared Macedonia to be 'the national state of the Macedonian people, providing for the full equality of citizens and permanent coexistence of the Macedonian people with

Albanians, Turks, Roma, and other nationalities'. Formerly, under the socialist constitution, the preamble defined Macedonia as a nation of 'the Macedonian people and the Albanian and Turkish minorities', and in 1991 Macedonian Albanians felt that they had been demoted as they were not explicitly mentioned as a constitutive nation along Macedonians.

As a matter of fact, during the 1990's the Macedonian political elites clashed with their ethnic Albanian counterparts over the basic idea behind the concept of the state. Various elements in the constitution, including the regulation of censuses, the laws on education, local self-government, and the public display of national minority symbols, the ethnic make-up of the police, army, as well as the public administration, were all contested by Macedonian Albanians during this period. These are all constituent parts of the idea behind the Macedonian republic, the fundamentals which in all liberal states are accepted by the general public or at least by each state's principal sectors.

Justice in liberal and ethnically heterogeneous states is provided if the state is not considered to be a 'nation-state.' In an ethnically divided society:

> "the state which treats every citizen as an equal cannot be a nation state: it must be a co-nation state. It cannot be identified with a single favoured nation but must consider the political community of all the ethnic groups living on its territory as constituting it. It should recognize all of their cultures and all of their traditions as its own. It should notice that the various ethnic groups contend with unequal initial chances for official recognition and a share of public authority, and it should offer particular assistance to the members of disadvantaged groups in approaching a position of equality. The privileges which are meant to countervail the initial disadvantages are inevitably lasting (since the inequality of the relationships of force between the state-forming groups are also lasting) and they might need to be expressed as rights" (Kis 1996: 224-5).

A pluralist state is more legitimate where more of its citizens, and not only the majority, regard the territory of the state as own homeland, the legal system of the state, its institutions and the insignia of the state as their own symbols. These are goods to be jointly shared with all of the other citizens. The political community of a liberal democratic but multicultural country will be just if:

> "it is formed from a union of ethnic groups living together. Its official symbols, holidays, its cultural goods handed down in school, and its historical remembrance will absorb something from the tradition of all the ethnic groups belonging to it, so that everyone can see the state is also theirs: likewise, everyone can see that the state is not their exclusive

possession but is held jointly with the other ethnic groups forming it" (Kis 1996: 237).

In this context, the demands by the Macedonian Albanians can be interpreted as being in favour of just such a union. Indeed, when one looks at the claims put forward by political representatives of the Macedonian Albanians one finds many which are well-suited to a just framework of relations within a multi-ethnic state. In the last ten years, the key demands of the Macedonian Albanians which have been a bone of contention with the central government are: reform of the constitution, greater representation of Macedonian Albanians in the civil service, the provision of university education in Albanian and decentralisation of state power.[14] Certainly, reforms have been enacted and improvements made as the participation of the Macedonian Albanians in civil society has risen over the past years. Similarly, a law has been passed allowing for private education in languages other than Macedonian, while a European-financed trilingual university (Albanian, English, Macedonian) was opened in 2001. However, these changes have not been sufficient for the political parties of the Albanians in Macedonia.

While Macedonians have continued to insist on a unitary nation-state, Macedonian Albanians have refused to be considered an ethnic minority within a Macedonian nation-state and have called for official bi-nationalism. Although Macedonia has recognised the rights of national minorities and promoted pluralism in the media, mother tongue education, minority civil society organisations, and inter-ethnic power sharing in the national government, living standards have sunk as unemployment soared. Under these circumstances the political transformation was formulated as a zero-sum game, pitting ethnic Albanian grievances against Macedonian fears for "their" country's security and integrity. With a major segment of the population challenging the very foundations of the state, before the 2001 Ohrid Framework Agreement and the subsequent adoption of the amendments to the 1991 constitution, Macedonia was not in a position to consolidate its democracy.

---

[14] See, for example, the reports by the International Crisis Group. 1999. *Towards Destabilisation?* ICG Balkans Reports No. 67 (May 1999), Skopje/Brussels, and *Macedonia's Ethnic Albanians: Bridging the Gulf*, ICG Balkans Reports No. 98 (August 2000), as well as Farimah Daftary. 2001a. "Testing Macedonia". *ECMI Brief # 4.* European Centre for Minority Issues, Flensburg and 2001b. "Conflict resolution in FYR Macedonia: Power-sharing or the 'civic approach'". *Helsinki Monitor*. no. 4.

Despite the unresolved inter-ethnic questions, Macedonia surprised analysts and diplomats when a full-blown civil war almost broke out in the first half of year 2001. Led by Ali Ahmeti, the previously unknown National Liberation Army (NLA) was a motley band of former Kosovo Liberation Army fighters from Kosovo and Macedonia, Albanian insurgents from the Southeast Serbian regions of Preshevo, Bujanovac and Medvedja, young Albanian radicals and nationalists from Macedonia, along with foreign mercenaries. From February to August 2001, the NLA organised an armed insurrection against the Macedonian government. Following prolonged skirmishes and with emotions running high among government officials, ordinary Macedonians and Macedonian Albanians, the danger of civil strife was real. The international community, led by the European Union, reacted swiftly, establishing the Ohrid Framework Agreement and achieving the pacification of the NLA.

What did the Framework agreement stipulate? The main goal of the Ohrid Agreement was to accommodate the grievances of the Albanian community, while at the same time preserving the unitary character of the state, thus addressing the concerns of the Macedonian majority who feared a ‘federalisation’ of the country and its eventual disintegration. The agreement envisioned a series of political and constitutional reforms designed to address ethnic Albanian demands for equal status. Consequently, the amendments to the 1991 constitution based on this agreement clearly illustrated the rights of national minorities, and especially ethnic Albanians. The major provisions include: amending the preamble to the Constitution, instituting double-majority voting in parliament, increasing the representation of ethnic Albanians in the police force, and stipulating the use of the Albanian language in official proceedings. Other provisions from the Ohrid Agreement call for the fulfilment of many of the demands raised by the Macedonian Albanians throughout the 1990’s and introduced some features of power sharing: this for instance included a system of double majorities requiring, for key parliamentary decisions, the consent of minorities represented in parliament, a substantial degree of municipal decentralisation, equitable representation of non-majority communities in the civil service, as well as confidence-building measures to overcome the immediate consequences of the 2001 conflict.

Effectively, the legal changes based on the Ohrid agreement clearly set out the rights of national minorities, and in particular of ethnic Albanians. On a symbolic level, a significant step forward was made when changes to the constitution were approved in November 2001 by the political representatives of Macedonian Albanians. Macedonia's ultimate source of legal authority is now legitimised in the eyes of ethnic Albanians. Other provisions of the Ohrid Agreement called for the fulfilment of many of the demands raised by the Macedonian Albanians throughout the 1990s. Having resolved the dispute over the character of the country, and following the new government's implementation of the provisions of the Framework Agreement, it is assumed that Macedonian Albanians, as a significant and crucial group of citizens in Macedonia, will not have an interest in disobeying the institutions of the state and that democratic consolidation has been largely accomplished.

4. Independent Kosovo: Implications for Macedonia

To what extent should Macedonia be concerned with the new status of Kosovo and the independence of its northern neighbour? Certain events since the birth of Macedonia in 1991, such as the Bit Pazar riots in 1993, the clashes surrounding the opening of the "University of Tetovo" in 1994, as well as the so-called Gostivar flag riots in 1997 indicate that inter-ethnic conflicts may indeed post a danger for the vitality of the Macedonian state. Since a significant number of Albanians in Macedonia are closely related to the Kosovar Albanians, one can imagine the apprehension among many Macedonians, especially since many young Macedonian Albanians joined the ranks of KLA fighting the Serbian forces during the war in Kosovo in 1999, while villages on the Macedonian border with Kosovo became logistical bases. For Macedonians there is a strong feeling that 'inter-Albanian' informal organisation transcends international boundaries. The popular view holds that this solidarity results from a shared ideal of the creation of a Greater Albania.

Indeed since Albanians living in Macedonia are closely related to Albanians in Kosovo, there is a strong and important link between political developments in Macedonia and Kosovo. Nationalist discourse makes us believe that for Albanian radicals the current Kosovar territory does not coincide with the imagined border of the "liberated", "great", Albanian state. The main question concerning Macedonian stability is therefore what kind of repercussions an independent Albanian Kosovo has on the inter-ethnic relations in Macedonia? Should Skopje fear the Albanian nationalism which resulted in Kosovo becoming a sovereign state? Could there be a repeat of the warlike crisis that hit Macedonia in 2001?

The answer is clear. Macedonia's leadership should not be worried by Kosovo's independence. This is mainly because the conditions and factors which led to the outburst of ethnic violence in Macedonia in 2001 are not prevalent at the moment. Some major issues have been modified or resolved. The interplay of internal and external factors that led to the outbreak of a mini-war in the winter of 2001 can hardly repeat itself now.[15] Macedonia is a more mature inter-ethnic democracy and an EU membership candidate country.

There are a number of reasons supporting this assessment. Let us briefly discuss the outbreak of hostilities in the winter and spring of 2001. As previously discussed, Macedonian Albanians and their political leaders have since independence fought for specific political rights for their ethnic community, including changes to the constitution. When in 1998 the Social Democratic Alliance, then a coalition partner of the Party for Democratic Prosperity, lost power, many Macedonians hoped that both economic conditions and the inter-ethnic relations would improve. Ethnic Albanians assumed that their political demands would be fulfilled. Three years later, many of them were dissatisfied since the largely corrupt government coalition between VMRO-DPMNE and DPA had not fulfilled the expectations of the Albanians in Macedonia for faster reforms that would improve their position.[16] In early 2001, a number of young Albanians from Macedonia were radicalised to the extent that they were ready to fight for the nationalist cause.

Some of these young Albanians either directly or indirectly participated in the war in Kosovo in 1999, the logistical networks of which were still functional in the winter of 2001. The routes for the transfer of weapons or soldiers across the borders in the triangle between Kosovo, Macedonia and Southern Serbia were still open at that time.[17] Many Albanians across the border in Kosovo were ready to help their brothers in Macedonia. In addition, in early 2001, Serbian security forces repelled armed Albanian rebels from the regions of Preshevo and Bujanovac,

---

[15] See more in depth in Zhidas Daskalovski *Walking on the Edge: Consolidating Multiethnic Macedonia 1989-2004*, Globic: Chapel Hill, 2005 or ibid, *The Macedonian Conflict of 2001: Between Successful Diplomacy, Rhetoric and Terror,* Studies in Post-Communism Occasional Papers, St. Francis Xavier University: Antigonish, 2004.

[16] See for example, Brenda Pearson, "Putting Peace into Practice: Can Macedonia's New Government Meet the Challenge?" (*US Institute for Peace Special Report*, November 2002) or International Crisis Group, "Macedonia's Public Secret: How Corruption Drags The Country Down", *Europe Report* N°133, 14th August 2002.

[17] See for example Robert Hislope "Between a Bad Peace and a Good War: Insights and Lessons from the Almost-War in Macedonia," *Ethnic and Racial Studies*, v.26, n.1, (January 2003).

adding new possible recruits for staging an uprising against Macedonia. By coincidence, at that time Macedonia signed a border agreement with the Federal Republic of Yugoslavia. Since the agreement also confirmed the border between Macedonia and Kosovo, it was understood by Albanians in these regions as a kind of a provocation. The agreement was especially unnerving for those Albanian groups which objected to a well-defined border because of their clandestine activities across the border.

A significant number of ethnic Albanian complaints called for leadership, which was easily found. Following the war in Kosovo, leading figures and one of the founders of the Kosovo Liberation Army coming from Macedonia like Ali Ahmeti, Fazli Veliu, did not win any spoils neither in Kosovo nor in Macedonia. Ahmeti and Fazliu were influential among the Albanian Diaspora in the 1990's and instrumental in gathering funds to finance the KLA's struggle. They and many Albanians from Macedonia who fought in Kosovo and Southern Serbia, but who personally gained little or nothing, had an interest in starting a moderately intense warfare in order to achieve benefits denied elsewhere.[18] Given also the availability of small arms in Macedonia, typically used for guerilla warfare, and the porousness of the border, it becomes clear why the war in Macedonia started in the winter of 2001.

Today in Macedonia there is no such confluence of factors. Although illegal weapons are still available to some extent, particular regions of the country are still hotspots, and radicalism among segments of the Albanian population is still strong, Macedonian Albanians enjoy the benefits of the reforms contained in the 2001 Ohrid Framework Agreement and subsequently implemented. All political elites accept the workings of the political system, despite occasional dissatisfactions with electoral results or the specific actions of particular governments. Despite the enlargement fatigue which has overcome Europe, Macedonia is firmly locked in to the path of EU integration, having been granted candidate status in the winter of 2005. Now waiting for a date to begin negotiations with the EU, Macedonia, as a unique multi-ethnic success story of the Balkans, has the support of the whole international community. These factors negatively influence the possibility of an outburst of new violence in Macedonia following Kosovo's achievement of the status of a sovereign state. Although it is not possible to give an absolute guarantee of such an

---

[18] See at Timothy Garton Ash, “Is There a Good Terrorist?”, *The New York Review of Books,* November 29, 2001 and in “Ali Ahmeti”, *Wikipedia, the free encyclopedia*, http://en.wikipedia.org/wiki/Ali_Ahmeti.

outcome, this analysis makes us believe that Macedonia should not fear the new independent status of Kosovo.

Conclusion

An independent and democratic Kosovo, recognised by Serbia, could be a great benefit for Macedonia. One could expect a stabilisation of politics in the region. Democratic Kosovo could become a generator of stability for Albanians in the Southern Balkans. Once the demands for independence have been satisfied, the more radical elements in Kosovo should be marginalised. The moderation of cross-border passions could serve well to teach a lesson to the militants among the Macedonian Albanians. Macedonian Albanians could become a strong link between Macedonia and Kosovo. Economic activity and exchange between the two countries would become ever stronger. Foreign investment would increase and so would the chances for the pan-European integration processes. The more the separation between Kosovo and Serbia is consensual and carried out in accordance with international law, the more this would bring stability in the region.

What are the implications for Macedonia? Paradoxically, the conditions for the stabilisation of democracy in Macedonia were met only after a bloody armed conflict in 2001 and the signing of the Ohrid Framework Agreement by all the relevant political parties in the country including DPA and PDP. The amendments to the 1991 constitution based on this agreement gave a clear picture of the rights of national minorities, including in particular ethnic Albanians. The Macedonian constitution is now legitimised in the eyes of ethnic Albanians. Other provisions from the Ohrid Agreement fulfil many of the demands raised by the Macedonian Albanians throughout the 1990s.

Macedonian inter-ethnic problems have largely been resolved with the passing and implementation of the Ohrid Framework Agreement. Although some issues remain open for discussion, the tensions over ethnic issues have been subdued since 2001. Moreover, there are no longer important segments of the Macedonian Albanian community which are ready to take arms to fight for political issues. Local Albanian elites have now all been in power and have accepted the democratic rules of the game. Having access to legitimate means of power and public resources, none of the elites is interested in undertaking (para)-military activities against the government. Yet while the repeat of the military crisis of 2001 in Macedonia is not expected, dangers remain especially if the independent status of Kosovo is not approved of by the international community as a whole and/or if the territory is partitioned.

References

Babuna, A., (2000), 'The Albanians of Kosovo and Macedonia: Ethnic Identity Superseding Religion', *Nationalities Papers*, vol. 28, no. 1, p.83

Brudar, M., (2006), "Kosovo i Metohija između htenja, realnosti i želja" in *Нова Српска Политичка Мисао* [New Serbian Political Thought] at http://www.nspm.org.yu/koment%202006/2006_brudar_kosovo22.htm .

Daftary, F., (2001)a, "Testing Macedonia", *ECMI Brief # 4*, European Centre for Minority Issues, Flensburg

—. (2001)b, "Conflict resolution in FYR Macedonia: Power-sharing or the 'civic approach'", *Helsinki Monitor*, no. 4

Daskalovski, Z., (2005), *Walking on the Edge: Consolidating Multiethnic Macedonia 1989-2004*, Globic: Chapel Hill

—. (2004), "The Macedonian Conflict of 2001: Between Successful Diplomacy: Rhetoric and Terror, *Studies in Post-Communism Occasional Papers*, St. Francis Xavier University: Antigonish

De Rapper, G., (1998) "Crisis in Kosovo: Reactions in Albania and Macedonia at the Local Level", *Ethnobarometer Programme Working Paper* No.3, Rome: CSS/CEMES

Fraenkel, E., (2003), 'Macedonia', *Nations in Transit 2003*, New York: Freedom House

Garton Ash, T., (2001), "Is There a Good Terrorist?", *The New York Review of Books*, November 29, 2001

Golubovic, Z., (2006), "Povodom izjave Tomislava Nikolića o proglašavanju okupacije Kosova-Opasan ratni poklič" in *Данас* [Danas] 15th February, 2006

Hislope, R., (2003), 'Between a Bad Peace and a Good War: Insights and Lessons from the Almost –War Macedonia,' *Ethnic and Racial Studies*, vol. 26, no. 1

International Crisis Group, (1999), "Towards Destabilisation?", *ICG Balkans Reports*, No. 67 (May 1999), Skopje/Brussels

—. (2000), "Macedonia's Ethnic Albanians: Bridging the Gulf", *ICG Balkans Reports*, No. 98 (August 2000), Skopje/Brussels

—. (2002), "Macedonia's Public Secret: How Corruption Drags The Country Down", *Europe Report*, N°133, 14th August 2002

Jackson, B., (2006), "Međunarodni faktori već odlučili da Kosovo ove godine dobije neki vid suvereniteta" in *Нова Српска Политичка Мисао*, [New Serbian Political Thought], http://www.nspm.org.yu/Debate/2006_KOS_dzekson.htm

Kis, J., (1996), "Beyond the National State", *Social Research*, 63:1

Pearson,B., (2002), "Putting Peace into Practice: Can Macedonia's New Government Meet the Challenge?", *US Institute for Peace Special Report*, November 2002

Rossos, A., (2002), 'The Macedonian Question and Instability in the Balkans', in Norman N. Naimark and Holly Case, eds., *Yugoslavia and Its Historians*, Stanford, CA: Stanford University Press

CHAPTER THREE

PUBLIC OPINION AND EU INTEGRATION: INFLUENCES ON THE POLICY PROCESS IN MACEDONIA AND IN THE EU

DANE TALESKI

Abstract

Public opinion plays a strong role in the creation and implementation of public policies. Important political issues animate strong public sentiments, focusing greater public attention on the issue and exercising greater pressure on policy makers. Nowadays, the EU integration process is one of the most important political processes in Southeastern Europe. On the other hand, in the political and public debate within the EU, the question of further enlargement raises a substantial attention. The aim of this chapter is to take the case study of one country and to explore how public opinion influences the process of the EU integration of that country. This country is the Republic of Macedonia. The influence of the public opinion will be explored on two levels:

1. how does public opinion in Macedonia influence the process of the integration of the Republic of Macedonia into the EU?
2. how does public opinion in the EU influence the process of the integration of the Republic of Macedonia into the EU?

Introduction

Desmond Dinan has tried in various articles to answer two important questions: why should a country join the EU and why should the EU be enlarged? (Dinan 2004:7-13). He points to a multitude of reasons why aspirant countries might want to join the EU, which is the basic motivation for them to pursue the EU integration process. Economic advantages rank high in the list, alongside with the wish to participate in the EU's common market. However, for some it has offered a chance to consolidate their democracies and to confirm their 'European' identity. For the countries from Central and Eastern Europe, which started their transition from the former regime at the start of the 1990s, it seems that all factors taken together played a role in strengthening the reasons for continuing with the EU integration process. Even though CEE and SEE countries faced high costs from the necessary reforms that had to be made to participate in the EU integration process, the long-term benefits were much greater. In this respect, for the countries in Europe experiencing transitional changes, the EU integration process was more a need than a choice that they have made. On the other hand, a basic motivation of the EU enlargement process is the promotion of stability and the enhancement of security in Europe. Therefore, even though enlargement as a process or as a political idea has not been strongly popular across the EU, the rationale behind it gives ample motivation for the continuation of this process. The EU enlargement also allows for growth of the EU's physical and economical space, allowing the EU to reflect wider interests and to play a stronger role in global political and economic relations (ibid:10-13). There are strong costs on the EU side flowing from the support for the EU enlargement process. These mostly relate to assistance to aspiring candidate countries, but also the allocation of a variety of resources to overcoming the division between the old members and the newcomers, a requirement in practically all the enlargement phases. With each successive enlargement phase, and especially for the enlargement towards Southeastern Europe, this feature only increases. However the processes of EU integration and EU enlargement are intertwined and present the two sides of the same coin. EU integration depends upon the reforms and policies made at the national level by the aspiring candidate countries, and EU enlargement depends primarily on the EU institutions as regards policy development, but also on the governments of the Member States concerning decision making. The processes of EU integration and EU enlargement go in parallel; they cannot be divided and should not be regarded as one sided, e.g., by considering one to be a continuation of the other. Ultimately, the policy outcome is the same for both processes: the addition of a new member to the EU. In that respect there is a strong synergy between EU integration and EU enlargement processes. Bearing this in mind, and for the purposes of this chapter, I will use interchangeably the expressions EU integration and EU enlargement throughout the chapter. I realise that they are distinct policy processes operating on different levels and involving different actors. However, as pointed out above, the policy outcome is the same for both. Moreover, my main interest is to see what, if any, the influence of the public opinion is on the two processes of EU integration and EU enlargement. I will not go in the details of the processes and specific policies associated with them. It is quite clear that they appeal to public opinion: EU integration appeals to public opinion in a specific country which is attempting to become an EU Member State, whilst EU enlargement appeals to the European public, i.e. to the public throughout the EU Member States. This is another common feature shared between the two processes.

However, when seen as policy processes, the differences between EU integration and EU enlargement processes are substantial. The process of EU integration is formulated and implemented at the national level, involving institutions and stakeholders of one specific country. Issues and interests may arise that go beyond the borders of the aspiring country, although the process of policy development and decision making is made within the context of the national political system. The EU enlargement process is more complicated. There are many complex issues and interests associated with the EU enlargement process. Stakeholders, who often have divergent interests, come from different countries and not always from EU Member States. The development of the EU enlargement policy is today rooted in the Maastricht Treaty, and, together with its management, is a matter left to the EU institutions. In this regard, EU enlargement falls within the supranational dimension of the EU. However decision making falls under the jurisdiction of the EU Member States, and in this regard it is a feature of the intergovernmental dimension of the EU. The EU integration process, as a national level policy process, interacts directly with public opinion. EU enlargement is a policy process that is a good reflection of the *sui generis* character of the EU, lying between the supranational and intergovernmental level. However, it attracts public interest both at the pan-European public level as well as in the different Member States.

1. The link between public opinion and public policy

The wealth of information in the public space provides for constant communication processes. According to Harold Lasswell, the communication process fulfils "three main functions in society: a) surveillance of the environment that provides warning about imminent threats and dangers to the system of values of a community or its parts; b) correlation of the parts of society in responding to the environment; and c) transmission of the social heritage from one generation to the next or cultural transmission" (Mattelart and Mattelart 1998: 29). In the political sphere the second function of the communication process is present on a daily basis. The political environment changes under the influence of different factors which resonate amongst the public. However in this process the public is not only the reflection of the changes, which is an inevitable outcome, but is also an important factor in influencing the changes in the political environment. In their work, Jeff Manza and Fay Cook (2002), after summarising the possible influence of public opinion on policy processes, suggest that the underlying logic regards the extent to which the influence is present, rather than the question as to whether there is any influence at all. Taking into consideration the existing literature on the opinion-policy link, they identify three sets of options: 1) public opinion has a significant and enduring effect on the policy process; 2) public opinion has a small and declining effect and 3) there are historical and institutional variations in responsiveness (Manza and Cook 2002). The proponents of the first option use mainly quantitative studies which show an "association between majority opinion and the adoption of new policies", while the proponents of the second believe that public opinion is weak on policy issues and thus it is constructed through polling and surveys (Manza and Cook 2002: 17). The third option is an intermediate approach based on a logic of "relativity". Namely, the proponents of this theory suggest that the influence of public opinion varies over space and time, and is specific to the policy dimensions. The three theoretical approaches are not in practice mutually exclusive, but rather combine and overlap. As my research in a specific policy dimension shows, the link depends on the importance of the policy for the public, and in this respect the link or influence may be strong or weak. On a general level, Manza and Cook find that the three theoretical approaches "reach fundamentally different conclusions that cannot be easily reconciled" (ibid: 28). I do not intend to argue either for or against such a conclusion, as I am not exploring enough cases and do not have sufficient variables on which to determine a supporting or contradicting argument. This chapter is locked on to one policy dimension, and that is the pivotal point rather than the overall link between public opinion and policy processes. I explore the EU integration/EU enlargement process and the links between this process and public opinion. The conclusions and outcomes have to be considered within that framework, rather then as starting point for a wider generalisation on the links between policy processes and public opinion. I will mainly explore the link between EU integration and EU enlargement and public opinion in Macedonia and in the EU. The data and conclusions from this part will be used as illustration for the second task of the chapter, which is to determine the influences of the public opinion on the EU integration and EU enlargement process. Here I am exploring the constellation of relations in Macedonia and in the EU.

My main case study revolves around the public opinion in Macedonia and in the EU. Therefore in order to proceed with exploration of the influences of public opinion in Macedonia, the EU and other countries on the EU integration and EU enlargement process, I shall first look at the 'trajectory of support' for EU integration and EU enlargement in Macedonia and in the EU. I draw the concept 'trajectory of support' from William Mishler and Richard Rose in their research on the public support for the post-communist transitions in Central and Eastern Europe and the former Soviet Union (Mashler and Rose 2002). The 'trajectory of support' in their work is taken as sets of public opinion data on approval of regime change in seven countries as indicators of the democratisation of those countries. The argument is that a high level of public support is an indicator of the legitimacy of the regime, although it also illustrates a capacity for policy creation and implementation. Leaning toward the theory of significant public influence, Mashler and Rose point out that "public confidence enhances the governments' abilities to make decisions and commit resources without resorting to coercion or the need to obtain citizens' approval for each and every decision" (Mashler and Rose 2002: 319). The authors imply that there is a correlation between the trajectory and dynamics of public opinion's support for a range of public policies and the creation and implementation of those policies. I will use this method of examination in order to determine public opinion's support in Macedonia and in the EU for the EU integration and EU enlargement process. Hypothetically, if public support for the policy process is strong, then this process will have stronger dynamics of implementation. Seen from another perspective, if public opinion is only weakly supportive, then the dynamics of the process will also be weak. The EU integration and EU enlargement process has its own specificities and therefore can not be regarded as any other policy process, as explained above. However the trajectory of support is an important indicator for the possibility of public opinion influencing the policy process. In this respect, providing an answer to the first research question on the trajectory of support for the EU integration and EU enlargement process is essential for proceeding with argumentation on the second research question concerning the influences of public opinion on the EU integration and EU enlargement process. In reaching conclusions on both questions, I use mainly data drawn from quantitative research, namely from survey results in public opinion polls.

This type of data has its own weaknesses, just as other research methods have their own strengths and weaknesses.

2. Public opinion surveys - reach and limitations

There are different quantitative and qualitative methods for researching public opinion (Brooker and Schaefer 2006; Norrander and Wilcox 2002). In this chapter, I will use data sets from quantitative studies of public opinion in the Republic of Macedonia and in the EU. The main method of quantitative studies is the public opinion survey, which can be conducted face-to-face, over the telephone, by regular post or over the internet. I have compiled two separate data sets, one for public opinion in Macedonia and the other for public opinion in the EU, both on issues of EU integration and EU enlargement. The data set for public opinion in Macedonia contains results from phone polls, while the data set for public opinion in the EU contains results from face-to-face interviews. The surveys in both cases have been conducted on a nation-wide representative sample (N=1,000 +) using probability sampling. While the poll results in Macedonia show the attitudes on a national level, the results for public opinion in the EU give the average of the results gathered in the surveys made in all EU Member States. In some cases there are differences between the Member States, which will be explored below. However where not specified otherwise, the results of the public opinion surveys in the EU show the average of the results gathered from all EU Member States.

Survey research is the method "used most often to learn about people's political opinions" (Brooker and Schaefer 2006:51). Polls are taken as a serious form of representation of peoples' views, despite their limitations. In a specific context, they reproduce the dominant framework of thinking and the main public rationale for a policy process or political issue. The power of their explanations is limited to the particular meaning of the set questions. Surveys are conducted mainly on sets of closed questions with pre-determined answers, where the respondents choose the option. However the "construction of meaning does not only occur in the space between question design and public response" (Lewis 2001:33). Once the data is gathered and the results are known they become the basis for social and political interpretation of public opinion. This is the starting point for measuring the influence of public opinion on policy processes. Besides opening up this possibility there are several other advantages of public opinion surveys (Brooker and Schaefer 2006:52). With careful random selection, the results from a given sample can, given a particular margin for error, be regarded as reflection of the public as a whole. The surveys are fast and relatively inexpensive, and when used properly public opinion surveys can describe the population or predict behaviour very accurately. One important advantage, especially for the purposes of this chapter, is that surveys use standardised questions that can be asked to many people in an identical form so that analysts can compare the answers received. In my research I depend on this approach, as I in principle use longitudinal analysis to determine the trajectory of support for the EU integration and EU enlargement process in Macedonia and in the EU.

Critics of public opinion surveys argue that they are superficial, the respondents do not have time to reflect and lack information, the responses are isolated and there is no equality among the respondents (Brooker and Schaefer 2006:53). Generally, surveys can not go into the subtlety of opinions, but rather describe how many people think what on a specific issue, without having the possibility to explain why. Usually the interviews (face-to-face or via phone) are limited in time, where the pollster speaks to respondents individually, thus allowing for the possibility of conformity of views or subjective bias. In all fairness, many of the respondents are not well-informed about the background to the issues or do not know well the context in which the questions are asked. In this respect people and their opinions are not equal. The discrepancies between the opinions and the knowledge of the people can be traced back to Plato, and his notions of *doxa* (opinion) and *episteme* (knowledge) which are seen as "properties of two quite distinct practices" (Lewis 2001: 15). The opinions undoubtedly stem from individuals' knowledge and there are different methods of measuring such knowledge. However in a political context, opinions create meaning. The connection between knowledge and opinions in the context of public opinion polls remains an open challenge, one that the polls can not always overcome. But in a political context people are strongly motivated by their opinions, and do not rely on their knowledge only to undertake supportive or confrontational action. Probably the most important limitation of public opinion polls is the length of time for which they provide verifiable results. This is due to the simple fact that people's opinion is susceptible to change. Change in public opinion occurs because reality changes or the perception of reality changes. There is also generational replacement, along with life cycle effects and manipulation by elites (Brooker and Schaefer 2006:206-211). Public opinion during the time that the surveys are conducted is merely a reflection of the events and processes at that time. Over time, events, mass movements or government policies make changes reality. Such changes, once accepted, cause a change in people's perception of reality. The generational replacement and life cycle effect occur due to the change of perception connected with the ageing of individuals, while the political elite is as much interested in knowing public opinion as in shaping it. In this respect the behaviour of the elites supports the view that public opinion matters in the political processes. However one must always be aware of the limitations and disadvantages of the methods of researching the public opinion, as elaborated in public opinion surveys.

3. Attitudes in Macedonia on the process of EU integration

The impact of EU integration and EU enlargement process on an aspiring candidate country is deep and profound. It has been noted that the process requires a "profound transformation of a country's laws, institutions, policies and orientations" (Grabbe 2003:257). In this respect the effects of the EU integration and EU enlargement process are seen in the trade between the country in question and the EU, domestic reform policies and the balance between the development needs of the country and the accession criteria. In some sense the effects are more of a normative nature, bringing changes to the institutional set up and approximation of legislation. However as many of these issues are part of the country's internal policy processes, they attract public attention and undoubtedly influence public opinion. The EU integration and EU enlargement process becomes part of the political life of the aspiring candidate country. In this respect the EU integration and EU enlargement process becomes "yet another actor in party competition" that "provides ammunition for many different sides in domestic political battles" (ibid: 259). Therefore there is a causal link between the EU integration and EU enlargement process and public opinion. The public in one country is interested in the prevailing policy processes, many of which are formed and fostered by the EU integration and EU enlargement process. In this study I am interested in verifying whether there is a feedback effect; in other words, does the public opinion influence the EU integration and EU enlargement process?

In recent years, public support for Macedonia's accession to the EU has been very high and stable. As can be seen from graph 1, from December 2003 to January 2007 the average level of support amongst citizens of Macedonia towards EU integration was between 87 and 92 percent of the total population. This represents the total of the answers from the public opinion surveys conducted over this period, from the end of 2003 to beginning of 2007, in relation to the question "If next week there were to be a referendum for entering the EU, how would you vote?".

Figure 3. 1 Support for EU integration in the Republic of Macedonia

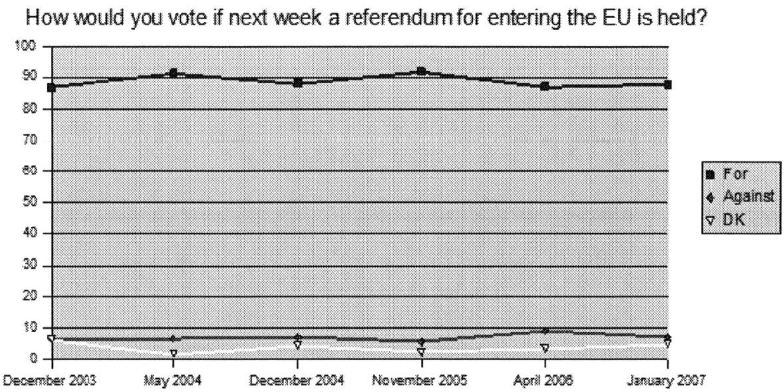

Source: IDSCS

In the same period of time only minor changes in attitudes are visible. The small peaks when the public support is the highest are in May 2004 and in November 2005. In May 2004 the already high support of 86.9 percent in December 2003, rose to 91.4 percent of the total population. Subsequently, in December 2004 the public showed a small decline in its support for EU integration, to some 88.2 percent. However this percentage again rose to 91.9 percent in November 2005. Throughout 2006 and at the beginning of 2007 public support has stabilised at 87 percent of the population. The percentage of the population that is against the idea of Macedonia joining the EU is quite low, at around 7 percent of all citizens. From the end of 2003 to the beginning of 2007, the variations in such attitudes reach a maximum of +/- 1.3 percent, with an exception in April 2006 when some 9.2 percent of the population was against joining the EU. This attitude declined to the now standard 7.2 percent in January 2007.

The support which the Macedonian public shows toward the EU integration process is very high and uncritical. A very low percentage of the population objects to this idea. The major developments in the EU integration process have some impact on enhancing the support; the peaks in public support seen in May 2004 and November 2005 coincide with the peaks in the dynamics of strengthening the relations between the EU and Macedonia. In April 2004, the Macedonian Government submitted its application to be accepted as a candidate Member State for joining the EU, and in November 2005, Macedonia received a positive opinion from the European Commission (EC), a so called positive *Avis*. The following month, in December 2005, this resulted in the decision of the European Council to give Macedonia the status of Candidate Country for joining the EU; a status that Turkey and Croatia already had, and which is formally the last step before a country joins the EU. The next step in the process of EU integration is becoming an EU Member State. The dynamics and progress of the EU integration of Macedonia may give pause for reflection on the part of the public, but does not substantially change the established attitudes of the citizens towards this process, which are strongly positive.

Macedonian citizens are not satisfied with the country's EU integration process. Some 60 percent of the total population reports this attitude between the end of 2003 and the beginning of 2007. Practically the same percentage of answers reflecting negative developments in the EU integration process is apparent in December 2003, April 2006 and January 2007: on average 60 percent. This percentage substantially lowers in May 2004, to 52.2 percent, and in November 2005, to 52.8 percent. However in the intervening period, as tested in December 2004, the perception of the people that the process of EU integration in Macedonia was going in the wrong direction increased to 58.8 percent. The summary of the results concerning the views of the citizens in Macedonia on the progress of the country's EU integration process can be seen in graph 2.

Figure 3. 2 Attitudes on the progress of the Macedonian EU integration

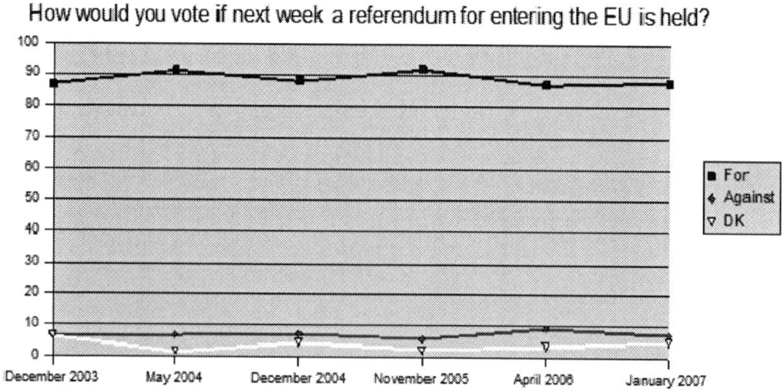

Source: IDSCS

The percentage of people who consider that the EU integration process is going in the right direction is also quite stable - between 35-39 percent of the total population. In December 2003, 39 percent of the population said that the EU integration process which Macedonia is undertaking is proceeding in a positive direction. This percentage dropped to 36.4 in April 2006, and 35 percent in January 2007. In May 2004, 46 percent of the population, an all time high, thought that Macedonia's EU integration was going in a positive direction, and in November 2005 the 44.4 percent that agreed with this view was almost 8 percent higher compared to December 2004. Again, changes in public opinion concur with the dynamics of the EU integration process. A lower score in the negative image of the EU and an increase in the positive one came when the Macedonian Government applied to become a candidate country and when the country received a positive response from the EU. There is a slightly stronger reaction to the actions of the national Government, as opposed to the reactions of the EU: there is a 2 percent difference within the positive image, with 46 percent of people stating that the EU integration process was going in the positive direction after the Government applied to become a candidate country, while 44 percent of the people agreed following the positive reply from the EC.

When it comes to the areas that should be given priority by the Government in the process of the EU integration, the citizens of Macedonia show similar views and attitudes. The overwhelming consensus can be easily seen in graph 6. The graph shows the results of the answers between December 2003 and January 2007.

Figure 3. 3 Priority areas for the integration of Macedonia

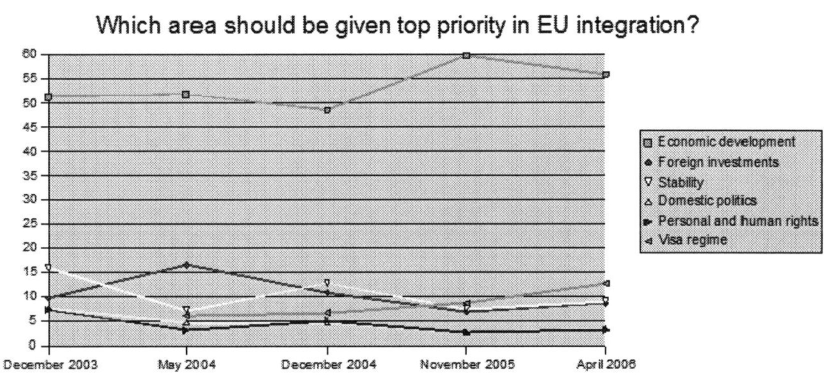

Source: IDSCS

Starting from December 2003, 51.3 percent of the total population agree that the economic development should be the top priority of the Government in the process of EU integration. While this percentage dropped to 48.5 in December 2004, in the last two years, by the end of 2005, it had *risen* to 59.8 percent, reaching 55.9 of the total population in January 2007. The other priorities are reflected by much lower percentages of the population and are susceptible to change over the time. For example, in December 2003 peace and stability was the second most important priority advocated by close to 16 percent of the population, in May 2004 over 16 percent opted for foreign direct investments, whilst nowadays over 12 percent of the total population agrees that the most important priority is the liberalisation of the visa regime that the citizens of Macedonia face when trying to travel abroad. In conclusion, there has been very little development in the views of citizens concerning which area should be given a top priority in the process of EU integration. For a majority of citizens the economic development of the country is a paramount obligation in the EU integration process. This attitude has amplified after Macedonia received the status of EU candidate country. This trend is not dependent, by and large, on the dynamics and developments of the EU integration process of the Republic of Macedonia.

The citizens of Macedonia not only agree on the main priority area in the EU integration process but also have the same expectations on the effects of this process on the aforementioned areas. Namely, when asked whether the influence from EU integration will be positive or negative in some of the areas mentioned, the majority agree that the effects will be positive. From December 2003 to January 2007, survey results have scarcely changed. All of them are plotted together and are presented in graph 7. The results show the expectations of positive developments in certain areas flowing from the process of EU integration that Macedonia is undertaking.

Figure 3. 4 Expectations in Macedonia for positive developments in certain areas from the process of EU integration

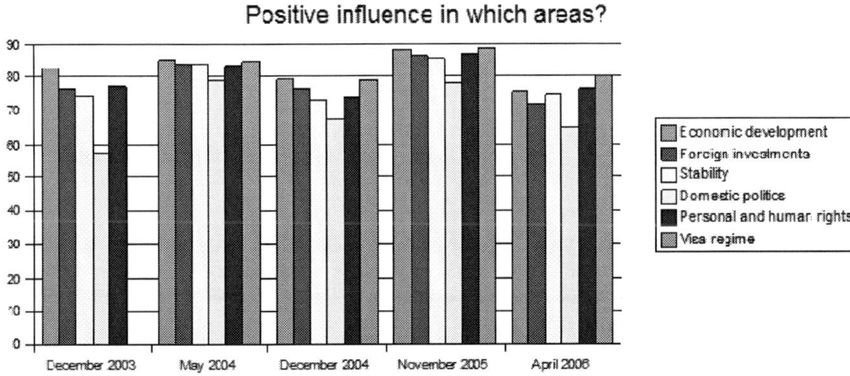

Source: IDSCS

From December 2003 to January 2007, the results range from mid 70 percent to close to 90 percent of the population that expects positive effects in the areas of economic development, foreign direct investments, peace and stability, personal and human rights and the visa regime. It seems that the economic development, together with the visa regime, attracts the most benevolent views from citizens. These areas have the highest concentration of answers expecting a positive development at all times. A small exception is the area of domestic politics, which has lower rates of expectations for positive developments. It ranges from 57 percent in December 2003 to 65 percent in January 2007. Even though it is lower than the other areas, positive expectations overcome other answers. It seems that citizens' expectations from the EU integration process are mainly that positive developments will occur. These positive developments mostly relate to freedom of movement and economic growth, and with a positive impact on the national politics meaning the sovereignty of the country. In any case, it seems that none of the trends is closely related to the dynamics and developments of the EU integration process in the Republic of Macedonia. It seems that following the application and confirmation of candidate status, these trends have slightly amplified, but have not substantively changed, and to a significant extent are not affected by the actions of the Government or of the EU institutions, with respect to the EU integration process of the Republic of Macedonia.

Public opinion in Macedonia relating to the EU integration process is concentrated both in direction and substance. The vast majority of the public supports the process. There is also a high concentration in the answers listing the priorities in this process and a high concentration of common answers relating to the expectations from the EU integration process. At the same time, the majority of the public is not very satisfied with the progress of the process, reflecting the opinion that more tangible results have not been achieved. In this respect, public opinion displays a capacity to influence the policy process of EU integration. It would be safe to say that the EU integration process is high on the public agenda, and that the public has a strong interest in seeing a dynamic process that provides tangible results mainly in terms of the faster integration of Macedonia into the EU and the socio-economic improvement of everyday life. As such, public opinion forces the EU integration process higher up the public policy agenda, leaving no space for any relevant actor to bypass the issue.

4. Attitudes in the EU on the process of EU enlargement

The analysis of public opinion in the EU concerning the enlargement process was undertaken approximately at the same time as that relating to Macedonia. The analysis starts from mid 2003 until the end of 2006. It covers mainly the EU level, meaning all EU Member States by the end of 2006, excluding Romania and Bulgaria. The analysis also compares and contrasts the attitudes of the citizens in the older Member States (EU 15) and the new Member States (NMS) that entered the EU in 2004. The analysis covers the support and the arguments in favour of enlargement, the expectations from, and the interests for, enlargement, as well as the attitudes which citizens throughout the EU have with respect to the possibility of Macedonia joining the EU.

Generally throughout the EU, the majority of the population supports the EU enlargement process. After the 'Big Bang' enlargement with 10 new Member States in 2004, such attitudes have become more widespread, and over 50 percent of the population across the EU supported further enlargement up to mid 2006. By the end of 2006 support had dropped to around 46 percent. At the same time, from mid 2003 until the end of 2006 the opposition to further enlargement also grew, reaching 42 percent in December 2006. Currently, support and opposition to the EU integration process are almost equal throughout the EU, as can be seen in graph 5.

Figure 3. 5 Support for the EU enlargement in the EU

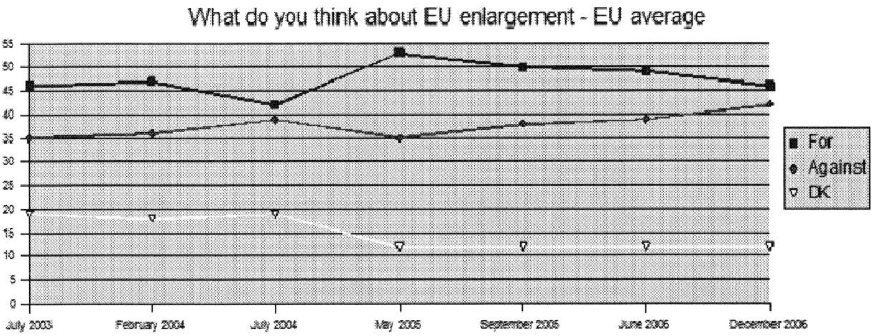

Source: Eurobarometer

It seems that after the 2004 enlargement round, the idea of future EU enlargement is loosing support, even though a slight majority of the population supports it. At the same time, opposition to future enlargement of the EU is steadily growing. Graph 6 shows the results of support for the EU integration process in the old (EU 15) and the new Member States (NMS). In a way it, shows the contrast between the EU 15 and the NMS, but also confirms the above conclusion.

Figure 3. 6 Enlargement support in the old and new Member States of the EU

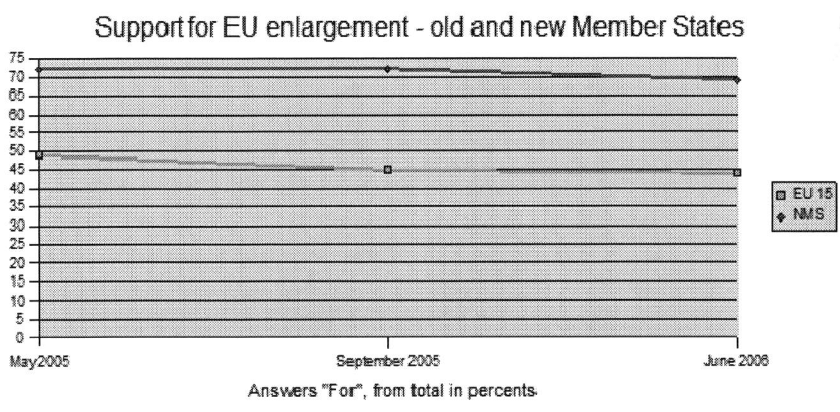

Source: Eurobarometer

There is a gap between the support for the enlargement process in the EU 15 and the NMS. While close to 70 percent of the population in the NMS supports enlargement, in the EU 15 only 44-45 percent agree that enlargement should continue. From May 2005 to June 2006, support for further enlargement in the EU 15 fell by some 5 percent. At the same time, support in the NMS, whilst remaining high, is also dropping by around 3 percent from May 2005 to June 2006. These data on one hand confirm the previous conclusion that support for enlargement across the EU is decreasing, but also show that public support for enlargement is much lower in the EU 15 than in the new Member States. Other research also shows that "with few exceptions, citizens of new Member States are more favourably inclined towards integration than the average in the EU 15" (Beichelt 2004:60).

The data in table 1 below provide additional arguments for similar conclusions. In particular, some of the old EU Member States, including founder members, have expressed lower than average support for enlargement for a longer period. This indicates that there is not a strong correlation between support for previous enlargement rounds and future enlargement in some of the older EU Member States. The point is that the 2004 enlargement could have been a turning point for the decrease in overall support for enlargement across the EU. However, in some of the Member States of the EU 15, public support for enlargement was lower than average even before the enlargement in 2004.

Table 3. 1 Support for enlargement in some EU Member States (the EU 15) in percentage terms

Enlargement support	July 2003 average: 46	February 2004 average: 47	July 2004 average: 42	May 2005 average: 53	September 2005 average: 50	June 2006 average: 49	December 2006 average: 46
Austria	43	41	34	28	31	29	31
Germany	42	38	28	36	33	36	30
Belgium	38	43	31	50	50	47	46
UK	36	38	38	50	48	43	36
France	31	34	37	39	32	31	34
Luxembourg	/	45	37	38	33	31	32

Source: Eurobarometer

In all of the Eurobarometer reports analysed, a majority of the EU Member States support the enlargement process at that particular point in time. However the most prominent support comes from countries which have gone through this process, rather than from founder members or early adherents. For example, in July 2003, February 2004 and July 2004 Eurobarometer, Greece was the most prominent supporter of enlargement with support from respectively 71, 65 and 66 percent of the total population. After joining the EU in 2004, Poland was the top supporter in May 2005 with 78 percent of its total population, and again in December 2006 with 76 percent. Another strong supporter of enlargement has been Slovenia, which came first in September 2005, with 79 percent of its population supporting enlargement, the highest percentage in the EU, and 74 percent in December 2006. A country will be more willing to support future EU enlargement if it has gone through such a process in its recent past. In other words newcomers to the club are more willing to invite new members.

However, no one in the EU wishes to press ahead with new enlargement rounds. Only limited sections of the Member States' citizens (irrespective of the date of entry of their state into the Union) now see enlargement as the main priority for the Union. Things have substantially changed since the 2004 enlargement round. This round of enlargement had a significant effect on the perception of priorities in the EU's enlargement process. The data in graph 7 present the results from July 2003 to June 2006.

Figure 3. 7 Attitudes in the EU towards enlargement as a top priority of the Union

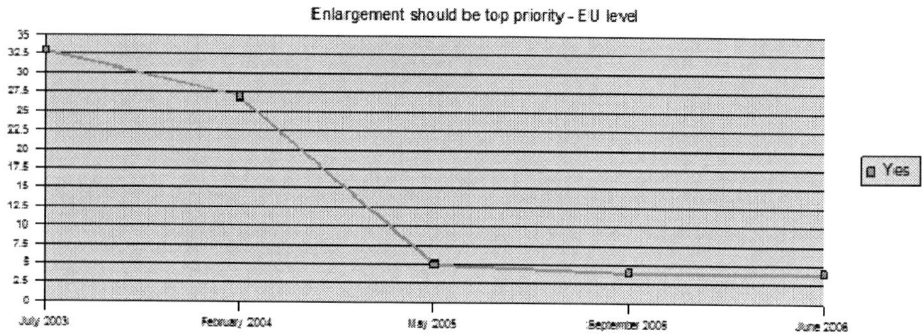

Source: Eurobarometer

It is very clear from the graph that the enlargement process became less of a priority after the 2004 enlargement. In July 2003, 33 percent, one third of the citizens of the EU, considered enlargement as the most important priority. By February 2004, this percent had dropped to 27 percent, falling yet further by May 2005, all the way down to 5 percent. Between the end of 2005 and the end of 2006, only 4 percent considered enlargement to be the top priority for the EU. This explains the current difficulty which the EU has in considering new enlargement rounds. After the enlargement in 2004, practically no one in the EU sees another round of enlargement as a main priority. This leads to the conclusion that in the near future public support for another EU enlargement is unlikely to increase. A high majority of the people both in the old and in the new Member States will not support new enlargement rounds any time soon.

It is very interesting to note that when considering future enlargement rounds, the majority of the EU citizens contemplate them in terms of enhancements of certain shared values across the European continent, some of which are most strongly found in the EU Member States. The results in graph 8 show the five main arguments that are supported by the vast majority of the citizens throughout the EU, when asked why the EU should continue with its enlargement process.

Figure 3. 8 The main arguments for EU enlargement before and after the 2004 enlargement

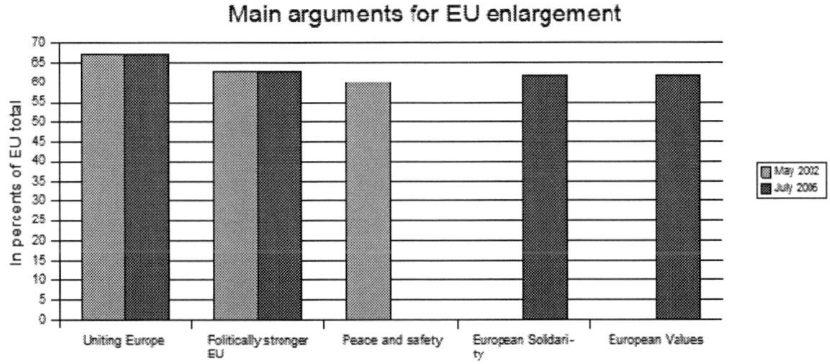

Source: Eurobarometer

Peace and stability in Europe is the main, overarching idea of the EU project, and the majority of the citizens (some 60 percent of the total population) see it as a strong argument for further enlargement. Other arguments claim that enlargement enhances the EU's strength, both internally and externally. 63 percent states that after enlargement the EU is regarded as being politically stronger, and an even higher percentage, 67 percent, agrees that enlargement unites the European continent. Other arguments offered in July 2006 include some vague political and moral concepts, such as European solidarity and European values, which normally refer to democracy, the rule of law and respect for human rights. It seems that for the majority of citizens across the EU the arguments in favour of enlargement are related to the effects and needs of the EU as a political project. Enlargement is good because of its political aims, and not so much because of its underlying economical rationale behind it.

The results presented in graph 9 provide additional arguments in support of the view that for the EU citizens the main rationale for enlargement is political and not so much economic. The graph shows the results of surveys in May 2002 and July 2006, before and after the 2004 enlargement round, in which the citizens reflect on the main conditions for future EU enlargement. The graph shows only answers on issues considered "very important".

Figure 3. 9 Most important condition for the process of EU enlargement, before and after the 2004 enlargement

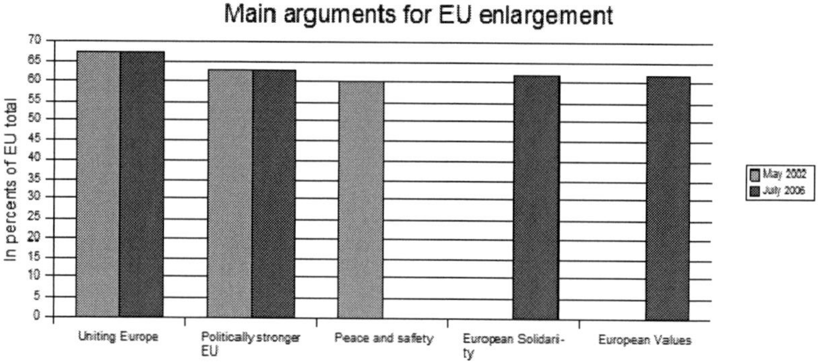

Source: Eurobarometer

Democracy and human rights are the main conditions that have stood the test of time, and are regarded as being just as important in July 2006 as they were in May 2002 with 73 percent of the population in 2006 and 79 percent in 2002. In May 2002, several other conditions were also indicated, such as the fight against organised crime and trafficking (76 percent) and respect and enforcement of EU rules (69 percent). Other more socio-economical conditions were also considered important in 2002, including respect for the environment, the need to keep down the costs of enlargement and the fact that the country in question was a net contributor to the EU budget. The economic development of the country was regarded the least important condition in May 2002. By July 2006 however, the economic development of the country had become the most important condition for entering the EU, coupled with respect for the rule of law, namely adherence to and enforcement of the EU rules and the fight against organised crime. Therefore one can conclude that compliance with the EU's political conditions is regarded by the citizens as the main test, both before and after the 2004 enlargement. Other conditions that have recently been crystallised include economic requirements and respect for the rule of law by the country in question.

Most EU citizens do not see enough clear grounds for and interest in promoting future enlargement. Results from the July 2006 Eurobarometer special study focused on future EU enlargement into the Western Balkans (WB) show this. Some of the results, considering the motives and interests, can be seen in graph 10.

Figure 3. 10 Attitudes in the EU on the interests of future EU enlargement with Western Balkans (WB) countries

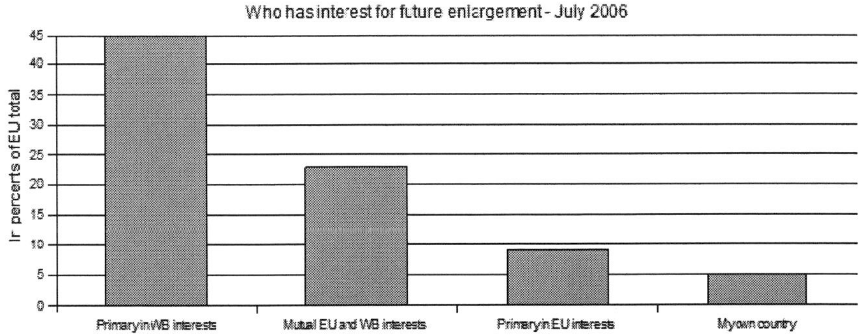

Source: Eurobarometer

The results show that for a majority of EU citizens, 45 percent, future enlargement would primary be in the interests of the Western Balkan countries. Some 23 percent see mutual interests between the EU and WB countries, while only 9 percent think that the EU has more of an interest in integrating the WB countries, with 5 percent stating that their own country would gain most following a new enlargement round of the EU into WB countries. This data give a rational explanation for the fact that future enlargement is not seen as an important priority for the EU. A majority of citizens think that the EU or their own country do not have sufficient interests to promote future EU enlargement with WB countries.

To conclude this part of the paper, I now turn the focus of my analysis towards the broader context of public opinion throughout the EU. Sufficient data can be found in the Eurobarometer reports to observe and analyse the public support in the EU for the membership of the Republic of Macedonia and its prospects of joining the EU. The data spans from November 2001, some time before the 2004 enlargement, up to July 2006. In addition to considering the general level of support, comparative analysis of the support from new and old EU Member States will also be made. In this regard, graph 11 shows the variations of public support across the EU for membership of the Republic of Macedonia.

Figure 3. 11 Support in the EU for Macedonia becoming an EU Member State

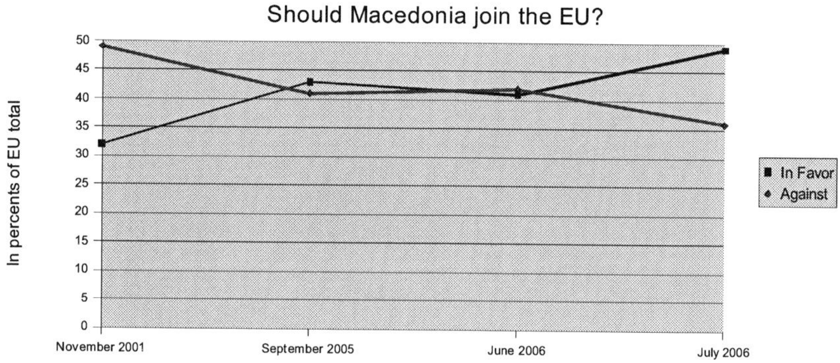

Source: Eurobarometer

In November 2001, a majority of the citizens in the EU, 45 percent, were against the idea of Macedonia joining the EU, while 32 percent of the population supported the possibility. By September 2005 the percent against had dropped by 8 percent to 41 percent, while those in favour rose by some 11 percent. In this manner, in September 2005 those in favour and those against the idea of Macedonia joining the EU were practically identical as a percentage of the total population. There was a 2 percent difference in favour of those who supported Macedonia. By June 2006, the 2 percent difference moved in favour of those against the idea of Macedonia joining the EU. At this time, while 42 percent of the EU population supported the idea of Macedonia joining the EU, 44 percent were against that idea. However a deeper enlargement study in July 2006, a special Eurobarometer focused on enlargement, showed that there was in fact strong support for Macedonia's adherence to the EU. According to this study, almost half of the population across the EU, 49 percent, supported the idea of Macedonia joining the EU. At the same more than one third, or 36 percent, were against this idea. The results show a growing tendency for support of the Republic of Macedonia joining the EU across the EU. At the same time, there is a tendency for public opposition to the EU integration process of that country to decline. While the initial change of support for Macedonia could have resulted from the 2004 enlargement frenzy, after 2005 support most probably derives from the dynamics and development of the EU integration process of the country. Since the end of 2005, the Republic of Macedonia has been a EU candidate member, which gives it a qualitatively different status in relation to future EU enlargement.

The growing public support for the EU integration of the Republic of Macedonia is even more visible when one turns to the results displayed in graph 12. They display the change of support for Macedonia's EU integration, but illustrate a split between the support coming from old and new Member States.

Figure 3. 12 Support for Macedonia joining the EU in the new and old Member States

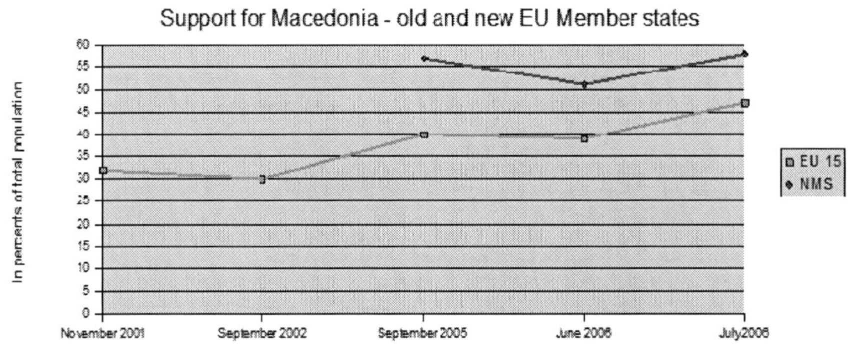

Source: Eurobarometer

Support in the old Member States remained at around 30 percent up to September 2002. However this support rose by 10 percent tin September 2005, to 40 percent and has steadily grown to 47 percent in July 2006. Across the new Member States, Macedonia has some 57-58 percent support from citizens as a whole, a level of support which subsequently fell to 51, but rose again to the level of support after Macedonia received the status of a candidate country. The conclusion is that the new Member States show a higher level of support for Macedonia joining the EU than the old Member States, although support in both is growing. Following the actions of the EU institutions, the positive *Avis* from the EC and the decision of the EU Council, support for Macedonia has grown. Irrespective of the fairness of such conclusions, there are also some very typical attitudes relating to who is in favour and who is against Macedonia's accession. Strong support comes from neighbouring or geographically chosen countries which have recently passed through the EU integration process themselves (Slovenia), with objections on the part of the public appearing in those countries which already have a proven track record in objecting to the enlargement process (Austria, Germany and Luxembourg).

While public support for EU enlargement is in decline, especially when considered as a potential priority for the EU, the focus of public attention has shifted to the quality of the process in terms of political gains for the Union. Still the views of the citizens are largely shaped by their nationality and recent experiences with EU enlargement, and only to a lesser extent by their sense of Europeanness. As such it is more likely that they will influence their national governments in relation to EU enlargement issues than the EU institutions.

5. Trajectory of support and public opinion influences on the EU integration/EU enlargement process

Support for the EU integration process in Macedonia has been high and stable, between 87 and 92 percent of the total population, from December 2003 to January 2007. Over the same period of time, support for the EU enlargement process in the EU has been between 46 and 53 percent of the total population. The dynamics of public support follow the dynamics of the processes. Namely as the Macedonian EU integration process intensified, so public opinion became more positive, and in the EU as a whole public support for enlargement reached its peak after the 2004 EU enlargement with 10 new Member States. Recent developments show that the public remains strongly supportive in Macedonia, while across EU it is in decline. Across the EU there is little interest in EU enlargement, in 2005 and 2006 only 4 percent of the population thought that this should be a top priority area. At the same time, a majority of the public in the EU considers that future enlargement will be to the benefit of the aspirant countries. Public opinion in the EU also shows a significant shift in interest toward the political gains of future EU enlargement. Public opinion in Macedonia sees EU integration mainly as an opportunity for economical development, and uncritically expects positive developments in other political and social areas. Surprisingly, the majority of the public is not satisfied with the progress of EU integration, which in turn raises expectations and creates frustrations. In this manner the high public expectations place a significant public focus on EU integration as a policy process.

The trajectory of support for the EU integration and EU enlargement process is high and stable in Macedonia, and stable and declining in the

EU. However there is a big difference in the level of support for the EU integration and EU enlargement process in Macedonia and in the EU. There is a 40 percent difference between public support in Macedonia and public support in the EU. While only some 10 percent of the public in Macedonia opposes EU integration, some 50 percent in the EU are against the EU enlargement process. There is also a strong discrepancy in the EU between public support for the enlargement in the old and in the new Member States. The dynamics of the EU integration and EU enlargement process has had influence on public opinion both in Macedonia and in the EU. In Macedonia there is strong public support for the process and which mainly focuses on economic issues and overall benefits. In the EU support is declining especially in terms of the priority it enjoys, and tends to focus on the political gains for the EU from the enlargement process. In this respect public opinion in Macedonia has more potential to influence the EU integration process, namely as regards the intensification of the process and the focusing of the process on the economic aspects. In the EU there is less scope for exercising influence, or for intensifying the process, but more on focusing the process on the political aspects. In this respect the influence of public opinion on EU enlargement differs across the EU Member States. The progress of the EU integration and EU enlargement has brought greater public pressure to bear in Macedonia to speed up the process and reap the economic gains, while the experience of the EU has made the public wary and has crystallised public interest around the political stability of the EU and the aspiring candidate countries. Public opinion seen as factor of influence on the EU integration and EU enlargement process in Macedonia pushes for faster integration and economic developments, while in the EU it pushes for a cautious approach and for the paying of greater attention to the political criteria.

As noted above, the EU integration and EU enlargement process have different structures. EU integration is a national policy process, while EU enlargement operates between the supranational and intergovernmental elements of the EU. On the national level, public opinion in Macedonia influences policy development and decision making towards faster implementation of the reforms needed to conclude EU integration. In this particular strong attention is paid to economical reforms, or more specifically economical development. The high public support combined with the strong dissatisfaction with progress creates pressures on the government to devote more time and energy to meeting public expectations. On the other hand, EU enlargement as a policy is developed by the supranational institutions and decision making occurs on an intergovernmental level. Public opinion in the EU is not cohesive enough concerning EU enlargement to influence the supranational level. On a supranational level, the policy development of the EU enlargement process is likely to continue following the dynamic and logic of the EU supranational institutions. However public opinion places a low priority on EU enlargement and focuses on political criteria. This will be reflected on the intergovernmental decision making level, which will have an effect on the overall policy process. The limited influence of public opinion in the EU mostly has an impact on the intergovernmental decision making level. The influence is varied, depending on the Member State in question. However public opinion will not generally speaking push national governments to speed up the EU enlargement process, although it may exert a certain influence in support of the importance of the political criteria which the aspiring candidate countries need to achieve. It should be quite clear, due to public opinion and the structure of the EU integration EU enlargement policy processes, that the public opinion will be a stronger factor in the EU integration policy process in Macedonia than across the EU and in the EU enlargement process. However the influence in both cases depends heavily on the interaction between public opinion and the national governments. In both cases the EU integration and EU enlargement process has influenced public opinion in Macedonia and in the EU, and there are feedback effects on both. The respective feedback effects in Macedonia and in the EU are contrasting and divergent. The feedback effect on the influence of public opinion on EU integration results in a drive for faster progress focusing on economic issues, while the feedback effect on EU enlargement entails a slowing of the pace with an increased a focus on political issues.

Conclusion

There is evidence pointing to a low level of a European identity and also there is little empirical evidence to show "the potential viability of Europe-wide policy discourse" (Gabel and Anderson 2004:14). Participation of the public in EU policy making processes is absent even in processes that are more coherent, i.e. are fully under the control of the EU institutions. The policy space within the EU is not strongly structured and thus public discourse does not always play a meaningful role. As institutional reforms in the EU are looking for ways to remedy this shortcoming, the influence of mass behaviour in the near future will be sought in other more coherent areas of EU policy making. The results of public preferences across the EU for EU policies show that they are not random. The interpretation of public preferences to is largely "similar to the interpretation of the EU policy space at the party group level" (ibid: 30). In this respect, public attitudes towards EU policy processes can be mapped out on the left/right axis as well as the supranational/intergovernmental axis. The EU enlargement process probably does not differ from other policy processes. The attitudes of the public probably vary according to their ideological differentiation and according to their stance on the supranational/intergovernmental dimension. Since the EU enlargement process is dependent both on the supranational and intergovernmental features of the EU, the potential influence of the public becomes even weaker. In this respect public opinion can influence the position of the national government in a specific Member State concerning the EU enlargement process. Given the structure of the EU enlargement policy process and the mapping out of public opinion preferences concerning this process, it is difficult to point to the influence that the EU public as a whole has on the EU institutions concerning the EU enlargement. On a national level, public opinion in various Member States can influence the position towards EU enlargement. In such cases public opinion may display a general preference for the EU enlargement, but is also dependent on conditions in the aspiring candidate country in question. In this sense one would expect greater public sensitivity across EU Member States toward the status of a aspirant country in its integration process, the progress of that process and the respect paid to the political criteria of the integration process.

Support for the EU integration process in Southeastern Europe has been predominantly high and uncritical. Research shows that it is mainly due to the "highly volatile context, in all likelihood, lack of information and experience in evaluating market-based issues purely on the basis of their costs and benefits" (Rohrschneider and Whitefield 2006:7). The public in Southeastern Europe sees the EU integration process as an instrument for the consolidation of democracy and development of market economies. But the strongest motivation in that respect is constituted by the economic expectations for integration, and in that sense EU integration is supported out of utilitarian views (Pippidi 2006). In line with Central and Eastern European countries, Southeastern European countries show a great interest in EU issues during the integration process when it is run as a national policy process, although once they become part of the EU they become less participative. Future developments and research will determine whether such a conclusion will also apply to Macedonia. In its current phase of the EU integration process, Macedonia seems to be moving along the same path as the other countries from SEE that have recently joined the EU. The 'Europeanization' effect is introducing rapid changes to the legal, political, legislative and economic systems. However the soft side of the 'Europeanization', including the adoption of values and democratic practices, is lagging behind. The strong support for the EU integration process is coupled with dissatisfaction and possible frustration with the progress of that process. Alongside expectations for positive benefits, mainly in economic gains, it creates a grave political climate. Public opinion will pressure the government to pay strong attention to the rapid progress of the EU integration process. However, that is mainly motivated by the expectations of economic benefits. What will happen in a situation where the government manages to achieve progress in the EU integration process, e.g. start negotiations for accession, but where there is no economical or other social progress? At the same time how will the public demands in Macedonia for faster EU integration focusing on economic developments even out with the public demands across the EU for cautious enlargement focused on satisfying the political criteria? And how will the public in Macedonia react when the costs of EU integration are incurred, such as for example the loss of national sovereignty?

The experience from other SEE countries shows that "public attitudes towards integration, and their interaction with the democratic process in post-communist states, differ in politically significant ways from other integration experiences in established democratic and market environments" (Rohrschneider and Whitefield 2006:241). The EU and Macedonia might discover interesting pointers in previous cases that would be beneficial for the on-going EU integration and EU enlargement process. In any event it will be interesting to compare the on-going developments of the influence of public opinion with the similar experiences of SEE countries that recently joined the EU.

References

Brooker, R., and Schaefer, T., (2006), *Public Opinion in the 21st Century*, Boston: Houghton Mifflin Company

Beichelt, T., (2004), *Die Europäische Union nach der Osterweiterung*, Wiesbaden: VS Verlag für Sozialwissenshaften/GWV Fachverlage GmbH

Bulmer, S. J., and Radaelli, C. M., (2005), 'The Europeanization of National Policy' in Simon Bulmer and Christian Lequesne. Eds. *The Member States of the European Union*, Oxford: Oxford University Press, pp. 338-360.

Dinan, D., (2004), 'The Road to Enlargement', in Desmond Dinan and Maria Green Cowles. Eds. *Developments in the European Union 2*, New York: Palgrave Macmillan, pp. 7-25.

Gabel, M. J., and Anderson, C. J., (2004) 'The Structure of Citizen Attitudes and the European Political Space', in Gary Marks and Marco R. Steenbergen. Eds. *European Integration and Political Conflict*, Cambridge: Cambridge University Press, pp. 13-32.

Gallagher, T., (2003), 'The Balkans Since 1989: The Winding Retreat from National Communism', in Stephen White et al., Eds., *Developments in Central and East European Politics 3*, New York: Palgrave Macmillan, pp. 74-92.

Grabbe, H., (2003), 'The implications of EU Enlargement', in Stephen White et al., Eds., *Developments in Central and East European Politics 3*, New York: Palgrave Macmillan, pp. 253-269.

Lewis, J., (2001), *Constructing Public Opinion*, New York: Columbia University Press

Manza, J., et al., (2002), *Navigating Public Opinion*, Oxford: Oxford University Press

Manza, J., and Cook, F.L., (2002), 'The Impact of Public Opinion on Public Policy: The State of the Debate', in Jeff Manza et al. Eds., *Navigating Public Opinion*, Oxford: Oxford University Press, pp. 17-33.

Mattelart, A., and Mattelart, M., (1998), *Theories of Communication*, London: Sage Publications

Mishler, W., and Rose, R., (2002), 'Public Support for Post-Communist Transitions in Central and Eastern Europe and the Former Soviet Union', in Barbara Norrander and Clyde Wilcox. Eds., *Understanding Public Opinion*, Washington: CQ Press, pp. 319-343.

Norrander, B., and Wilcox, C., (2002), *Understanding Public Opinion*, Washington: CQ Press

Pippide-Mungiu, A., (2006), 'East of Vienna, South of the Drina: Explaining the Constituencies for Europe in Eastern Europe', in Robert Rohrachneider and Stephen Whitefield, *Public Opinion, Party Competition and the European Union in Post-Communist Europe*, New York: Palgrave Macmillan, pp. 165-187.

Rohrachneider, R., and Whitefield, S., (2006), *Public Opinion, Party Competition and the European Union in Post-Communist Europe*, New York: Palgrave Macmillan

Appendix: Data used for the public opinion analysis

1. Republic of Macedonia

For the analysis of public opinion in Macedonia, the database of public opinion polls of the Institute for Democracy "Societas Civilis" - Skopje (IDSCS), titled "Public perceptions of the process of EU integration and the EU institutions in Macedonia" was used. IDSCS has conducted surveys on a nation wide representative sample (1,000 - 1,200 respondents) in:

- December 2003,
- May 2004,
- December 2004,
- November 2005,
- April 2006, and
- January 2007.

The research was carried out in cooperation with the Secretariat for European Affairs of the Government of the Republic of Macedonia. All survey results are available at www.sep.gov.mk

2. European Union

For the analysis of public opinion in the EU, the database of the Eurobarometer public opinion polls published by the European Commission was used. Surveys are conducted on the basis of nation-wide representative samples (1000 respondents) in all Member States, as well as in candidate countries. The Eurobarometer is published in several versions: Standard, Special and Flash Eurobarometer. For the purpose of this paper the following Eurobarometers publication were used:

Standard Eurobarometer

- Eurobarometer 59, "Public Opinion in the European Union", Spring 2003
- Eurobarometer 60, "Public Opinion in the European Union", Autumn 2003
- Eurobarometer 61, "Public Opinion in the European Union", Spring 2004
- Eurobarometer 62, "Public Opinion in the European Union", Autumn 2004

- Eurobarometer 63, "Public Opinion in the European Union", Spring 2005

- Eurobarometer 64, "Public Opinion in the European Union", Autumn 2005

- Eurobarometer 66, "Public Opinion in the European Union", Autumn 2006

Special Eurobarometer

- Eurobarometer 251/ Wave 65.1, "The Future of Europe", May 2006

- Eurobarometer 255/ Wave 65.2, "Attitudes Towards European Union Enlargement", July 2006

- Eurobarometer 56.3 "Special Bureaux" *Getting Information on Europe, the Enlargement of the EU & Support for European Integration: European Public Opinion Takes the Floor*, May 2002

The research materials, survey reports, technical and methodological notes can be accessed at http://ec.europa.eu/public_opinion/index_en.htm

CHAPTER FOUR

EUROPEANIZATION AND THE INSTRUMENTALITY OF IMPOSING A MINORITY DISCOURSE: REFLECTIONS ON BULGARIA'S AND OTHER CEE NEW EU MEMBER AND CANDIDATE COUNTRIES' EXPERIENCE

PLAMEN RALCHEV

Abstract

This chapter argues that the minority discourse constitutes an integral part of the Europeanization discourse, given the experience of oppressed and frustrated minorities (like Roma) in Central and Eastern Europe. The aim of the chapter is to consider and discuss the instrumentality of the application of rational and/or constructivist institutionalist approaches to Europeanization, explaining the mechanism for imposing and operating the minority discourse as part of the overall processes of European integration and the Europeanization of domestic politics, as well as its immediate implications for the polities and societies in SEE.

Introduction

Like the countries of Central and Eastern Europe which joined the EU in 2004, the countries in SEE have been passing through processes of transformation in the hope that they will eventually become EU members.

Notwithstanding their actual status – EU members or EU aspirants – the Balkan/SEE countries are all involved in a large-scale process of transformation, approximating European standards and practices. This comprehensive process is the essence of the Europeanization of the Balkans. In a nutshell, the Europeanization of the Balkans marks a bold effort at anchoring this region to the EU mainstream.

Europeanization in SEE, as well as in the countries of Central and Eastern Europe, is a broad process of adopting measures and mechanisms for fitting into the EU lines.

This chapter, however, will consider the process of Europeanization only as a context rather than a topic of research. The enquiry will focus on and attempt to explain a specific phenomenon which has occurred within the process of Europeanization. In my research I broadly label this phenomenon as 'imposing a European discourse' but I concentrate on a specific dimension of the European discourse, that is the minority rights discourse, which stems from the EU Copenhagen political criteria. In a broader sense, the minority discourse is part of a broader Europeanization discourse that previously motivated all reform and modernisation efforts in the Balkans, whether in the case of Bulgaria's and Romania's accession to the EU, or the stabilisation and association arrangements for the countries of the Western Balkans.

In recent years the EU, alongside other European organisations such as the Council of Europe and the OSCE, has turned into a cornerstone for minority rights protection in Europe. It is crucial to acknowledge the impact of these organisations in developing a framework of minority politics in Europe.

This chapter focuses on the meaning of the Europeanization discourse as a political, public and decision-making motivational tool, as well as serving as a political board (compared to the concept of 'currency board', effective in Bulgaria since 1997). The Europeanization discourse is considered here as a functional and institutional 'straitjacket' for national policy-makers and the public at large.

The minority discourse constitutes an integral part of the Europeanization discourse given the experience of oppressed and frustrated minorities (such as Roma) in the region, and even the history of inter-communal conflicts in the former Yugoslavia throughout the 1990s and in Macedonia in 2001.

The aim of this chapter is to consider and discuss the instrumentality of the application of rational and/or constructivist institutionalist approaches to Europeanization explaining the mechanism for imposing and operating the minority discourse as part of the overall processes of European integration and the Europeanization of domestic politics, as well as its immediate implications for the polities and societies in SEE. I will also discuss the agents who impose it and the internal and external repercussions of the application of this discourse.

1. Europeanization through Conditionality or through Discourse?

Most of the studies on the Europeanization of EU candidate countries are conducted within the framework of the institutionalist theory, and in particular, within the context of the debate between rationalism and constructivism.[1]

If we consider Europeanization as transformation and changes in domestic policies, practices and perceptions, one of the ways to explain it is either by following the 'logic of consequences', suggested by the rational institutionalist approach, or by using the 'logic of appropriateness'. The former maintains that "adaptational pressure from the EU changes the opportunity structure for utility-maximising domestic actors. It empowers certain actors by offering legal and political resources to pursue domestic change. Formal domestic institutions are the main factors impeding or facilitating changes in response to EU adjustment pressures."[2]

Alternatively, constructivist institutionalism argues that such responses follow the 'logic of appropriateness'. The EU's domestic impact results from a process of socialisation in which domestic actors internalise EU norms which they regard as legitimate.[3]

The present inquiry was prompted by the question as to whether either of these two approaches suffices to explain transformations in Central and East European and Balkan countries, in particular, on their path towards EU membership. By taking minority issues as an example of change, I argue that neither of the two approaches, taken separately, explains those transformations sufficiently. It is rather a merger of both approaches, or a more integrationist view, that seems to be more adequate in explaining changes in new EU Member States and applicant countries. To this end, I incorporate both the rational and constructivist institutionalisms in a line of argument that in fact claims that 'imposing a discourse' is a consequence of both domestic elites' rational choice and the socialisation of their preferences and choices through setting and communicating a particular discourse to the general public.

---

[1] Sedelmeier, U., Europeanization in New Member and Candidate States, Living Reviews in European Governance, CONNEX/NEWGOV,2006, p. 10

[2] Ibid.

[3] Ibid.

While rationalist institutionalism focuses primarily on the use of conditionality by the EU to influence candidate countries by affecting their material interests, constructivist institutionalists stress that the EU's impact depends not only on domestic material interests, but also on the "extent to which there is a 'cultural match' or 'resonance' between EU demands and domestic rules and political discourses."[4]

There is indisputably influential recent literature on discourse and policy changes in Europe. Whilst not claiming however to offer an extensive literature review on this research area, the chapter builds on the methodological stance of V.A. Schmidt (2001, 2002), U. Sedelmeier (2006), G. Sasse (2005) and Fr. Fischer (2003).

In Schmidt's view, *discourse* "represents both the policy ideas that speak to the soundness and appropriateness of policy programmes and the interactive processes of policy formulation and communication that serve to generate and disseminate those policy ideas".[5]

Gasper and Apthorpe (1996) provide a comprehensive overview of different approaches to policy as discourse. Their starting point is to see policy discourse as 'argumentation', rather than as objective and scientific statements. In other words, policies are ways of putting forward an argument about what a particular situation (or what the world) is like, and what should be done about it.

According to them, discourse analysis encompasses several strands. Some of the most important conclusions from these various strands of argument are that:

1. Policy discourse inevitably frames problems in a certain way, i.e. includes some aspects rather than others.
2. Policy discourse determines (and is determined by) a larger set of 'rules' about what is sayable and thinkable. This approach might focus more widely on the stories and narratives that sustain policies, and the explicit or implicit rules of validation.
3. Policy discourse is not 'just words' but has material effects, as a change in discourse will have an effect e.g. on the distribution of resources.[6]

---

[4] Ibid, p. 13

[5] Schmidt, V.A., C. Radaelli, Policy Change and Discourse in Europe: Conceptual and Methodological Issues, West European Politics, Vol. 27, No.2, March 2004, p. 193

[6] Gasper, D., Apthorpe, R.; Introduction: Discourse Analysis and Policy Discourse, European Journal of Development Research 8 (1) pp. 1-15, 1996

Fischer (2003) explains policy discourse as communicative interactions among political actors that translate problems into policy issues. He further quotes Schmidt (2001), who argues that "discourse can provide insight into the political dynamics of change by going behind the interplay of interests, institutions, and cultures" to explain how change is brought about by "an interactive consensus for change through communication" among the key political actors.

It is difficult to separate discourse from the interests expressed through it, or from the institutional interactions which shape their expression or the cultural norms that frame them. Discourse can exert a causal influence on political change, although the influence tends to be that of an intervening rather than an independent variable. For this reason, Schmidt explains that discourse cannot be ***the*** cause, but it is often ***a*** cause of political change.[7]

Two dimensions can be featured in Schmidt's approach: ideational and interactive. In ideational aspect, "discourse supplies policy with substantive arguments, both empirical and normative", thus providing for a particular policy discourse including reference to its "normative appropriateness in terms of broadly held social values".[8]

The interactive dimension of discourse refers to institutions and actors who carry out 'coordinative' and/or 'communicative' functions. Coordinative discourse relates to policy construction and development, and may include government agencies, epistemic communities, advocacy coalitions and discourse coalitions. The communicative function of the interactive dimension, on the other hand, refers to discursive exchanges with the broader political system and occurs in various deliberative policy forms. Prioritising certain policy issues, "its primacy function is to generate persuasion and confer political legitimacy on policy initiatives".[9]

---

[7] Fischer, F., Reframing Public Policy: Discursive Politics and Deliberative Practices, Oxford University Press, 2003, citing: Schmidt, V. A., The Impact of Europeanization on National Governance Practices, Ideas, and Discourse, Paper presented at European Consortium for Political Research Workshop on Policy, Discourse and Institutional Reform, Grenoble, France, 6-11 April 2001, and Schmidt, V.A., The Futures of European Capitalism, Oxford: Oxford University Press, 2002

[8] Fischer, F., Reframing Public Policy: Discursive Politics and Deliberative Practices, Oxford University Press, 2003, citing: Schmidt, V.A., The Futures of European Capitalism, Oxford: Oxford University Press, 2002

[9] Fischer, F., Reframing Public Policy: Discursive Politics and Deliberative Practices, Oxford University Press, 2003, p. 31

Table 4. 1The Interactive Dimension of Discourse

Function	Actors	Interlocutors	Generator of ideas	Purpose	Form
Coordinative	Policy actors	One another	Epistemic community, discourse coalition, advocacy coalition, policy entrepreneur	Construct policy program, come to agreement	Provide language and framework for policy actors' discussion and deliberation
Communicative	Political actors	Public	Policy actors, political entrepreneur	Communicate to public, provide orienting and legitimising	Translate program into accessible language for public discussion

Source: Schmidt (2002, p. 231*)*

While Schmidt prioritises constructivist discourse in the institutional context, or discursive institutionalism, rational institutionalism also tries to explain policy change induced by the process of EU integration.

Table 4. 2 Rationalist vs sociological institutionalism

	Rationalist institutionalism	**Sociological/constructivist institutionalism**
EU strategy	Conditionality	Socialisation
Facilitating international factors		
	clarity of EU demand credibility of conditionality sizeable rewards and power asymmetry monitoring capacity	identification with EU legitimacy of EU demands
Domestic facilitating factors		
Polity dimension	liberal democratic governments high quality of political competition at moment of regime change dominance of liberal ethnic policy preferences in parliament	positive normative resonance with domestic rules transnational (epistemic) networks
Policy dimension	low actor density/number of veto players internationalisation of policy sector absence of institutional legacies	

Source: Sedelmeier, U., Europeanization in New Member and Candidate States, Living Reviews of European Governance, CONNEX/NEWGOV, 2006, p. 11

2. Minority Protection as Conditionality and Discourse

The review of rationalist and constructivist institutional approaches intends to set the frame of reference for considering policy changes with regard to minorities in EU candidate countries.

In the cases of Bulgaria and Romania, as well as those of associated Western Balkan countries, changes of domestic perceptions and attitudes are induced primarily through external leverage. Therefore, it is reasonable to consider the rational institutionalist and constructivist institutionalist approaches for explaining policy changes in the new EU Member States and EU applicant countries as working simultaneously or sequentially rather than as alternatives to one another. This is because the two processes of European integration and Europeanization, as described by V.A. Schmidt, overlap in terms of timing, implementation and implications.

This chapter argues that a balance between external and internal incentives for change is needed in order for EU conditionality to work effectively. Conditionality is generally regarded as a major means of 'democracy promotion' and 'Europeanization' in Central and Eastern Europe.[10] Bulgaria and Romania, as well as the other Balkan countries, regardless of their status on the EU membership waiting list, showed that they are no exceptions. The minority rights aspect of the Copenhagen political criteria is just an example of how conditionality works in practice. As Sasse (2005) notes, "the combination of EU conditionality, the norm of minority protection and the context of post-communist transition make for a rich empirical testing ground".[11]

Of course, conditionality effectiveness varies from country to country and it is not the aim of this chapter to set out empirical findings, but rather to provide an overall assessment and conceptualisation of mechanisms for policy changes, especially with regard to minority issues. What I argue is that, regardless of country variations, the logic of policy change and policy transformations follow nearly identical algorithms. Stage 1 involves the setting of conditions for national decision-and-policy-makers for the adaptation of domestic policies and practices in line with the EU 'standards', the integrity of which is *a priori* beyond question. Guided by rational choice, those policy-makers have no other option but to stick to

---

[10] Sasse, G., EU Conditionality and Minority Rights: Translating the Copenhagen Criterion into Policy, EUI Working Paper RSCAS No. 2005/ 16, p. 4

[11] Ibid.

the rules if they are determined and serious about advancing on the EU membership track, or reaching the top position on the EU waiting list.

If we follow the reasoning of rational institutionalism, implementing Stage 1 should have been sufficient. However, domestic political processes make decision-makers vulnerable to shifts in public opinion and voters' attitudes and perceptions. Therefore, it is vital for the political survival of decision-makers to legitimise their rational choice policy decisions and to persuade the domestic public of the appropriateness of measures taken.

This shows the necessity of Stage 2 in which certain ideas and views are communicated to the general public in order to obtain public endorsement for policy changes. Thus, a specific discourse is established in order to justify rational choices made by governments or other decision-making bodies in line with the conditionality principle. Stage 2 fits in with the analytical framework of constructivist institutionalism. As suggested above, Stages 1 and 2 occur in virtually all new EU Member States and associated countries as complementary rather than mutually exclusive procedures.

The minority discourse has proved to be instrumental, especially in view of the conditional assistance which the EU provides to the SEE countries. The conditionality of assistance is intrinsically related to the very way in which a particular discourse happens to work - setting performance criteria and making them compulsory, raising public awareness about the necessity and benefits of these criteria.

As Sasse observes in her study, it is difficult to define "the exact relationship between domestic political incentives and EU conditionality in the area of minority protection". It is also difficult to distinguish between the synergism of effects of the EU, or organisations such as the OSCE and the Council of Europe, which also have a stake in minority protection. Nevertheless, Sasse resumes, "the timing of certain decisions, and the domestic political context of individual candidate countries provide insights into the effectiveness of EU conditionality, and more specifically, the conditions facilitating or limiting the EU's impact."[12]

It is evident that irrespective of the relevant policy change, its occurrence depends on the rational choice of governments and on public acceptance of this change. This provides a good reason for describing the induction of minority protection criteria in EU candidate states as the 'imposition of a minority discourse'. This concept covers both the rational choice of governments in accepting certain positive policy measures

[12] Ibid., p. 12

regarding minorities, as well as the government policy of persuading the general public about the acceptability, rationale and appropriateness of those measures. Since minority issues are a highly sensitive and contested policy area in Central and Eastern Europe, including in the Balkan countries, the communication of a minority discourse to the public majority is a serious challenge, as far as it affects perceptions, nationalist ideas, minority rights promotion, and last but not least, implies a redistribution or re-allocation of scarce public resources in favour of particular minority groups. The communication of his broad spread of policy aspects to the public and the need to convince it of the common sense behind such decisions, without provoking any backlash, is an impressive task that all governments and elites of transition countries face. They therefore have no option but subtly to impose minority-related decisions on the majority public by nurturing understanding and informed consent. Where governments fail to do so, they run the risk of implementing ineffective policy in the teeth of opposition from the majority public. Governments should persuade domestic majorities of the need to implement specially designed minority policy.

In their attempt to establish and sustain minority-assertive domestic environments, national governments join forces with external and domestic factors involved in imposing the discourse in question, including most importantly those who communicate the discourse – opinion makers, including domestic and international NGOs, and the media[13].

Transnational networks connecting candidate countries' elites with the EU are a facilitating factor in the EU's influence for both rationalist and constructivist institutionalist approaches.

Perhaps the most suitable example of how policy change is complemented by a targeted discourse setting concerns the Roma minority in Central and Eastern Europe, and especially the Balkan countries. In virtually all of the countries in the region, the promotion of Roma-affirmative policies has unleashed a public backlash and even extremist rhetoric and hate-speech. Therefore, the imposition of a minority discourse is a timely and responsible mission involving domestic and external factors.

---

[13] For a topical and detailed study on the specific case of Bulgaria's Roma and their media 'image', see Bakalova, M., The Role of the Electronic Media for the Integration of Roma, Open Society Institute Sofia, 2004

In this chapter I invoke the discourse on the Roma minority as illustrative of minority discourse because the Roma are the largest ethnic, social and structural minority in all Central and East European countries, including the Balkans. Moreover, they constituted a growing challenge for domestic elites and policy-makers during the process of transition and application for EU membership. Nearly all EU applicant countries have been criticised by the European Commission's annual reports due to their mistreatment of domestic Roma minorities, most of which lack any feasible modernisation prospects. It is not that Roma issues do not need special attention; they do. But the problem of the Roma's social inclusion and integration in polities and societies in transition has many dimensions. First, in order of priority, there is a critical stalemate in the political science perspective – how is it possible to accommodate modern and post-modern polities with the pre-modern strata claiming their legitimate place therein? Secondly, national governments and domestic policy actors are obliged to respond to incentives (and also pressures) coming mainly from the European Union, but also from other international organisations (Council of Europe, World Bank, OSCE), to implement and uphold an affirmative policy with regard to Roma minorities, in order to maintain EU membership as an achievable objective. In so doing, national governments in EU applicant countries adopt strategies and programs for the integration of Roma minority members and the improvement of their social status. To this end, they receive (conditional) support from the EU, as well as from non-governmental organisations such as Soros' Open Society, which together with the World Bank launched in 2005 an ambitious far-reaching initiative called 'The Decade of Roma Inclusion'. As I have discussed the appropriateness of that and similar initiatives in a separate paper[14], I shall refrain from going into depth on this topic. However, it is important to note that whatever policy changes and initiatives national governments may decide to undertake in favour of Roma minorities, thus keeping the possibility of EU membership open, they will have to justify their decisions before the general public. It is not enough to say, 'this is the EU condition. Take it or leave it.' If governments state their decisions in public in such terms, they will only instigate either further Euro-scepticism among their citizens, or, worse still, EU-antagonism and nationalist backlashes at home.

Therefore, as discussed above when comparing rationalist and constructivist approaches to explaining policy changes in countries in

[14] Ralchev, P., The Decade of Roma Inclusion – Affirmative Action in the New Europe?, 2005, www.iris-bg.org/Roma%20Decade.pdf

transition, it is not only domestic policy actors that have to accept those changes. Also the public and society as a whole need to be receptive. One of the subtle ways in which governments can do this is to employ the whole instrumentality of persuasion techniques, involving civil society resources, the media and a significant number of organisations, in imposing *the* discourse needed for the general public to become aware of the appropriateness and relevance of the changes at hand. Thus, EU conditionality ultimately becomes domesticated and, instead of an *imminent evil*, is regarded by general public as an appropriate rational condition.

As noted above, the EU is not alone in applying conditionality to the 'hopeful' countries. Other organisations, whether European, international, intergovernmental as well as non-governmental, follow the same line. As Sasse concludes, EU conditionality in the area of minority protection could be best understood as the "cumulative effect of different international institutions". She further continues, "the actual policy leverage of the EU in minority protection has been anchored in the instruments and recommendations of the Council of Europe and the OSCE, and a range of other actors, including NGOs, have translated them into the domestic political context."[15]

The process of imposing a minority discourse has formal and informal impacts. Formal impacts include institution-building along with the establishment of mechanisms and procedures for policy-making that are motivated to take into account minority concerns that may have been previously overlooked if not neglected. The informal side includes some critical changes in perceptions, attitudes and awareness of the majority public concerning minority grievances, a change, which marks at least a significant threshold, if not a breakthrough.

Conclusion

In recent years, a number of seminal studies have been published which analyse policy changes and transformations in countries applying for EU membership. Taking transformations in some Southeast European countries as a point of departure, and drawing on the methodological scholarship of rational and constructivist institutionalism as a framework of analysis, the chapter argues that policy changes and transformations in transition countries on the road to EU membership could be best

[15] Ibid., p. 18

understood and explained as a dual process (or a set of complementing processes) of rational choice decision-making and the communication and legitimisation of these decisions to the general public through the setting or 'imposition' of a particular discourse. Minority discourse within the context of EU enlargement and integration was taken as an example of how rational and constructivist institutionalist approaches could be employed in explaining various transformation stages occurring in EU candidate countries. However, it is important to remember that the imposition of any kind of discourse related to the EU is possible only if a candidate country has a credible accession perspective. In that case, the induction of a minority-conducive public discourse provides for the legitimisation of governments' policies pursued in line with the EU integration requirements and conditions.

On the whole, the chapter forms part of the latest tendency to conceptualise minority politics within the context of an expanding EU and the efforts of a group of scholars working in recent years on the formulation and cultivation of minority protection within the EU.

References

Bakalova, M., (2004), The *Role of the Electronic Media for the Integration of Roma*, Open Society Institute Sofia

Fischer, F., (2003), *Reframing Public Policy: Discursive Politics and Deliberative Practices*, Oxford University Press

Gasper, D., (1996), Apthorpe, R.; 'Introduction: Discourse Analysis and Policy Discourse', *European Journal of Development Research* 8 (1) pp. 1-15, 1996

Sasse, G., (2005), 'EU Conditionality and Minority Rights: Translating the Copenhagen Criterion into Policy', *EUI Working Paper* RSCAS No. 2005/ 16

Schmidt, V.A., C. Radaelli, (2004), 'Policy Change and Discourse in Europe: Conceptual and Methodological Issues', *West European Politics*, Vol. 27, No.2, March 2004

Schmidt, V. A., (2001), 'The Impact of Europeanization on National Governance Practices, Ideas, and Discourse', Paper presented at *European Consortium for Political Research Workshop on Policy, Discourse and Institutional Reform*, Grenoble, France, 6-11 April 2001

—. (2002), *The Futures of European Capitalism*, Oxford: Oxford University Press, 2002

Sedelmeier, U., (2006), 'Europeanization in New Member and Candidate States', Living *Reviews in European Governance*, CONNEX/NEWGOV, 2006

CHAPTER FIVE

THE EU AND THE WESTERN BALKANS: SAP AS AN INSTRUMENT OF REGIONAL STABILISATION

CLAIRE GORDON[1]

Abstract

The chapter explores the operation and impact of EU instruments and policies in facilitating the adoption and implementation of international standards pertaining to human rights and the rights of minorities in the post-violent stages of conflict in the former Yugoslavia (Serbia, Croatia, Bosnia-Herzegovina, Kosovo and Macedonia). It examines how the actions of the EU have interacted with the domestic political context in these countries in order to assess how far the EU has contributed to inclusive social and political approaches to conflict settlement agreements and the integration of minority communities. The chapter also considers where the actions of the EU together with other international organisations have worked in the opposite direction impeding processes of integration and leading to continued division and antagonism in the countries of the region.

[1] This chapter was written thanks to the generous support of the MIRICO project (Human and Minority Rights in the Life-Cycle of Ethnic Conflicts) under the VIth Framework of the European Commission. See http://www.eurac.edu/Org/Minorities/MIRICO/index.htm. I am grateful to Gwendolyn Sasse and Sofia Sebastian for their invaluable input into the preparation of this chapter.

Introduction

Almost from the first rumblings of restiveness in the former Yugoslavia in the late 1980s/early 1990s, the EC/EU sought to become engaged in the process of conflict management in the Western Balkan region though its early interventions were marred by weak conflict management capacities and inadequate political will. In the wake of the violent conflicts in Croatia, Bosnia-Herzegovina, Kosovo and the largely averted violent conflict in Macedonia, the EU has remained actively involved in keeping the peace and encouraging reconstruction and reconciliation all of which have been embedded in a process of broader rapprochement with the promise of eventual integration in EU. This chapter explores the evolution of the EU's Stabilisation and Association Process (SAP) as its primary approach to post (-violent) conflict management in the Western Balkans drawing on the apparently tried and tested instrument of conditionality for inducing political and economic stabilisation, transformation and integration into the EU. As part of its investigation of the SAP process, this chapter concentrates on the political aspects of stabilisation in post-conflict societies. Firstly, the EU's emphasis on a regional approach to conflict management is scrutinised in conjunction with the bilateral dynamics which have underpinned relations between the EU and states in the region. Secondly, the EU's approach to minority rights is considered in the context of fostering stabilisation and democratisation in the countries of Former Yugoslavia. In this way the chapter raises the fundamental question of how effective an instrument the SAP is for addressing the particular set of post-conflict transformation problems confronting the Western Balkan region.[2]

The EU has clearly been on a steep learning curve as it sought to carve out appropriate policy responses to the rapidly changing developments in the Western Balkan region in the course of the 1990s. It has developed new instruments in its attempt to accommodate the dual challenges of conflict and post-conflict management coupled with post-communist transition. In this it has been influenced by (i) its early failures in conflict management and in handling the complex shifts in majority-minority relations in the Former Yugoslavia in the early 1990s; (ii) the accession process of the eight Central and East European countries (CEECs) that entered the Union in May 2004 as well as the two Balkan states of Romania and Bulgaria that acceded in January 2007, a process which in the view of the Commission was fruitfully shaped by the pull

[2] Calic, 2005.

effect of conditionality; (iii) intra-EU developments which post-Maastricht have been influenced by the attempt to develop an effective second pillar in the form of the Common Foreign and Security Policy; and (iv) the lack of EU legal base and accompanying institutional capacity which would facilitate the meeting of the norm of 'respect for and protection of minority rights' in external countries.[3]

It is argued here that:

1. *On SAP and the evolution of conditionality*

The EU's approach to engagement in the Western Balkans region would appear to be based on enmeshing formerly conflicting parties in a set of contractual relations built on conditionality-based operating principles.[4] Though SAP has been significantly influenced by the CEECs enlargement process, through the introduction of additional stages and interim measures of conditionality, the EU has sought to prolong the potential effectiveness of the operation of conditionality as an instrument to induce compliance with political and economic stabilisation and reform programmes. Despite the firmer upfront guarantee of ultimate enlargement, through SAP the EU has also developed a means of drawing out the path to accession. The commitment to membership holds firm, but the time-frame remains indeterminate and the credibility of the conditionality is arguably lessened.

2. *On SAP and the regional approach*

Notwithstanding the professed primacy of 'good neighbourliness' and the importance of regional integration, the instruments of the SAP have basically been structured around the top-down bilateral country-by-country CEE accession-oriented model and have displayed similar and in some cases even more pronounced shortcomings given the post-conflict situation in the region. Notwithstanding certain modifications aimed at tackling the needs of stabilisation in the Western Balkans, the EU has had mixed efficacy in facilitating political and economic regional integration.

3. *On SAP and Minority Issues*

Despite the ostensible commitment to stabilisation encapsulated in the very name of the SAP instrument, the EU remains ill-equipped to stabilise

[3] For further discussion, see Casarini and Musu, 2007, Sasse, 2005 and Toggenburg, 2006.

[4] For an in-depth consideration of the EU's contractual relations in conflict situations see Tocci, 2007.

post-conflict minority-majority relations inside particular countries as well as across the broader Western Balkan region. A considerable mismatch persists in the EU between rhetoric, policy instruments and the funding of actual projects facilitating minority protection. This gap is underlined by the disparity between the understanding of 'respect for and protection of minorities' as per the 1993 Copenhagen political criterion and the actual challenges of operationalising this element of EU conditionality in post-conflict settings (in particular the implementation of minority-friendly policies and the building of capacities at the sub-national level). Moreover the approach of EU institutions to minority rights as one crucial aspect of post-conflict reconciliation has remained rather narrow; policy departures in this area have been markedly focused on refugee return and institutional reconstruction and there has been limited engagement in other important dimensions of minority rights.

All of this begs the question of whether the SAP constitutes a considered policy approach to post-conflict resolution or whether it approximates (1) an indirect trickle-down approach based on presumed peace dividends from delivering economic and social stabilisation and closer EU integration (2) coupled with fragments of more targeted policies including in the area of minority rights – even if these have been less clearly and specifically formulated. The 2007 round of progress reports which, with the possible exception of Croatia, appear to defer even further the prospect of full membership would suggest this might well be the case. Thus this chapter contends that the current approach to post-conflict management potentially poses serious dilemmas for future progress in the Western Balkans region, an area where the satisfactory resolution of inter-state relations and intra-state majority-minority relations must surely lie at the heart of any long-term political stabilisation process.

The current chapter first provides an overview of the evolution of EU policy towards the countries of the Former Yugoslavia from 1990 to 1999, from the lead-up to the outbreak of violent conflict to the NATO bombing in Serbia. This period was characterised by short-term reactive crisis management policies and is largely a record of an EU which was ill-equipped and unprepared to deal with the complex challenge of collapse, conflict and contagion in the Former Yugoslavia. Secondly the chapter considers the emergence and development of the Stabilisation and Association Process under the auspices of the EU as well as its relationship to the intergovernmental Stability Pact. The emergence of these two institutions marked a shift from an ad hoc 'fire-fighting style' of crisis management to a more long-term broadly integrationist approach to the Western Balkans region. Under this new incremental transformational strategy, which sought to expand the instrument of conditionality as applied to the CEECs, the states of the region were to be embraced in a comprehensive multi-stage framework fostering political and economic development together with enhanced regional cooperation all of which was to be underpinned by the prospect of EU membership at some point in the future. The evolving nature of SAP conditionality is explored as well as the underlying tension between regional integration versus the bilateral dynamic of interaction which has structured the organisation and delivery mechanisms of the SAP. In the third and final part of the chapter, the SAP and its instruments are assessed as tools for facilitating post-conflict reconciliation in the area of minority rights. The chapter evaluates the actual commitment of the EU to these different elements as well as the complementarity of different policy approaches in terms of facilitating the long-term domestic political stabilisation of the individual countries of the region as well as increased intra-Balkan regional integration.

1. Short-term reactive crisis management: EU Balkan Policy 1990-1999

'If one problem can be solved by the Europeans it is the Yugoslav problem…This is the hour of Europe, not the hour of the Americans.'
(President of Council of Ministers, Jacques Poos, 1991)

This statement of the then President of the Council of Minister Jacques Poos encapsulates the ambition which existed in certain quarters of the EC in the early 1990s to develop an independent foreign policy-making capacity and to carve out a role for itself as a key foreign policy player, a zeal which ran ahead of both available political will and available institutional resources in the case of the conflicts in the former Yugoslavia. The Maastricht Treaty which formalised the Common Foreign and Security Policy (CFSP) as the EU's second pillar was only approved in 1992 and fully ratified the following year when violent conflict was already underway in a number of the republics of the former Yugoslavia (FY).[5] Furthermore the conflicts in the FY escalated and descended into violence at a time when the international community was only edging

[5] Up until the establishment of the CFSP pillar in Article 17 of the Treaty of European Union at Maastricht, the foreign policy instruments of the EU were very limited. Wallace, Wallace and Pollack, 2000.

towards increased international (largely humanitarian) involvement in the affairs of sovereign states coupled with a shift to greater reliance on regional organisations for managing conflict processes. The disintegration of Yugoslavia was evidently related to the broader processes of post-communist collapse in Eastern Europe. But the international community and the EC/EU, which were preoccupied by the break-up of the Soviet Union with its massive nuclear weapons arsenal and unprepared for the end of the traditional bipolar broadly predictable two-bloc balance of power politics, were ill-equipped to deliver an effective strategic and institutional response to the unfolding events in South Eastern Europe.

Though there was early recognition that instability in the Balkan region would have negative consequences for broader European security and there was a resulting commitment to containing the conflict, the paucity of tools in the foreign policy arena, the limited prior focus on minority issues, and divisions of opinion among member states hampered the EC/EU's ability to respond effectively to the complex and evolving situation.[6] These shortcomings in political and institutional capacities meant that the EC/EU's early attempts at more active engagement in the conflict management arena were to end in failure, with the U.S. and NATO having to step in Bosnia, Kosovo and Macedonia.

The initial response to the deteriorating situation in Yugoslavia was managed by the EC's troika which organised a series of shuttle diplomacy peacekeeping missions to the region, and established the Peace Conference in The Hague to develop solutions to the evolving crisis with its attendant Arbitration Commission (the Badinter Commission) which was to provide legal advice and rulings on the complex issues of sovereignty and self-determination that were initially implicitly and then immediately at stake.[7] Much has by now been written on the failures of EC/EU peace-making through the instrument of the Conference in The Hague and the subsequent London Conference whose succession of peace plans failed to ward off and then silence the guns.[8] Likewise the evolving sanctions regime and the sequencing, timing and legal foundations of the EC/EU's recognition policy vis-à-vis the seceding states of the Former Yugoslavia has also been subjected to considerable scrutiny.[9] Time and again in the first half of the 1990s events on the ground ran ahead of decision-making processes and the attempt to follow due process in

[6] Phinnemore and Sianni-Davies, 2003, 172.
[7] Caplan, 2007; Wolff and Rodt, 2007.
[8] See, for example, Gow, 1997, Malcolm, 1996, Weller and Wolff, 2005, Woodward, 1995.
[9] Caplan, 2007.

Brussels leading the EC/EU to be accused of contributing to the process of Yugoslav disintegration.[10] Not only were there major difficulties in reaching consensus among member states but also in putting into effect credible incentives which would induce the warring parties to participate actively and with good will in peace negotiating processes. Despite the optimism of Poos, the EU's nascent conflict management skills were put to the test and found to be severely lacking. At best the EU's policy could be summed up as a case of reactive ad hoc crisis management.

The EU's attempts to strengthen its foreign policy dimension both in terms of capacities and common actions have in part been a response to the early failures in Yugoslavia. The inadequacy of EU responses to the shifting majority-minority relations in the process of collapse of the former Yugoslavia was also reflected in the inclusion of the minority reference in the first political Copenhagen criterion.[11] As the series of conflicts evolved and EU foreign policy instruments improved with the development of the CFSP in the wake of the 1999 Treaty of Amsterdam and the appointment of the High Representative, the EU was able to play a more positive role in allaying the excesses of violent conflict in FYROM (Macedonia) in 2001 and two years later in Montenegro where the process of peaceful separation became virtually synonymous with Javier Solana, the EU High Representative.[12] It also became increasingly clear that though it was important for the EU to develop its own independent defence capability, the Union could make a more positive contribution to conflict management in the post-violent conflict stages, building on its ongoing experience of using the tools of 'soft power' to induce third parties to stabilise politically and economically with the ultimate promise of EU integration.

With all the potential ambiguities of its operation, the instrument of conditionality with the ultimate reward of EU membership at the very least strengthened the domestic commitment to continued democratisation and

---

[10] According to Caplan, 2007, three sets of documents provided the framework for the EC's recognition policy: (i) the EC Conference on Yugoslavia's draft Convention of 4 November 1991 (the 'Carrington Plan'); (ii) the opinions of Badinter Commission; and (iii) the actual policy of conditional recognition adopted at 16 December Council of Ministers meeting and articulated in the EC' twin 'Guidelines on the Recognition of New States in EE and the SU' and the 'Declaration on Yugoslavia'.

[11] European Council (1993) Presidency Conclusions para. 7 (iii) Copenhagen European Council, 21-22 June. [Available at: http://europa.eu/european_council/conclusions/index_en.htm]

[12] Ulrich Schneckener, 2002 and Rory Keane, 2004.

marketisation in the CEECs.[13] This was in stark contrast to the EU's ineffective record of conflict management in the Western Balkans in the early 1990s. In the latter part of the 1990s the EU shifted to a different approach to conflict management in the Western Balkans in the form of the Stabilisation and Association Process. Drawing on its strengths the EU sought to promote enhanced association -- economic and technical assistance, promotion of trade and integration into EU markets -- as well as regional stabilisation through more proactive peace-building policies taking into account the specifics of the post-conflict setting in the countries of the Former Yugoslavia.

2. The emergence of the regional approach to post-conflict stabilisation

The origins of a more comprehensive regional approach to political stabilisation and economic recovery in the Western Balkans date back to the Royaumont Process (RP) which was launched with the aim of supporting the implementation of the Dayton Peace Agreement in December 1995. The RP involved EU members, South Eastern European Countries (SEECs), regional neighbouring countries, the United States, Russia, the OSCE and the Council of the Europe. The process was framed under the need 'to overcome divisions and differences and thus create at all levels of civil society the trust needed to build a network of good neighbourly relations between States.'[14] Its main objectives were (1) to encourage the normalisation of relations and foster political dialogue between Western Balkan countries; (2) to encourage people-to-people links and promote regional cooperation in the field of civil society and culture; and (3) to support the implementation of projects conducive to peace and stability, good neighbourliness and civil society.[15]

The regional approach was to provide itself with aid measures and a conditionality framework later on. In July 1996 the Obnova financial regulation was introduced to implement aid measures in the Western

[13] See Hughes, Sasse and Gordon, 2004; Grabbe, 2006 and Smith, 2003.
[14] Council of the European Union, 1998, Common Position of 9 November 1998, defined by the Council on the basis of Article J.2 of the Treaty on European Union, concerning the process on stability and good-neighbourliness in Southeast Europe. (98/633/CFSP). Available at http://eurlex.europa.eu/LexUriServ/site/en/oj/1998/l_302/l_30219981112en00010007.pdf
[15] Ibid.

Balkans. In the area of political stabilisation and democratisation, Obnova incorporated a democratic conditionality clause under which Balkan countries were requested to respect specific rather generally stated conditions defined by the Council.[16] The Council's conclusions on the principle of conditionality stated that 'assistance in support of democracy through Phare could be considered subject to evidence of a country's credible commitment to democratic reforms and progress in compliance with the generally recognised standards of human and minority rights.'[17] The regional approach appeared to be undermined by the fact that it was structured around bilateral delivery and assessment mechanisms, the tried and tested format for operationalising conditionality.[18] Moreover in the event most of the financial assistance provided by Obnova under the 'support of democracy' classification was directed towards operations aimed at reconstruction and refugee return, reflecting a rather limited commitment to supporting broader processes of democratisation.[19]

By 1997 the EU was also moving towards the application of conditionality in the Western Balkans; after all given its policy failures in conflict prevention and management in the first half of the 1990s, conditionality was one of the one few foreign policy tools among its limited panoply of external instruments which was delivering positive results albeit elsewhere -- in the Central and Eastern European countries. In April 1997 the Council formally adopted the Regional Approach outlining its conclusions on the application of the principle of conditionality in its relations with the countries of South East Europe.[20] The 1997 Regional Approach brought together marketisation, democratisation and regional cooperation (the 'establishment of good neighbourly relations'). However, from the outset a potential tension emerged between the priority attached to the regional dimension and the

---

[16] Ibid. Human and minority rights were specified as non-discrimination between citizens, and included the resettlement of refugees and displaced persons.

[17] Phare was originally created in 1989 to assist Poland and Hungary in the wake of communist collapse. In 1997, it was reoriented for candidate countries and tied exclusively to the goals of accession, primarily the preparation of the CEECs for the obligations of membership and in particular the tranposition of the acquis. See Mayhew for further details on Phare, 1998.

[18] Panebianco and Rossi, 2004, 4.

[19] See Article 2 of the Obnova regulation, Council of the European Union, July 1996.

[20] Council conclusions on the principle of conditionality governing the development of the European Union's relations with certain countries of south-east Europe', 29 April 1997, http://europa.eu/bulletin/en/9704/p202001.htm [accessed November 12, 2007]

actual organisation and operationalisation of the conditionality; financial assistance and trade preferences were conditioned upon compliance with a set of conditions laid out contractually in the form of bilateral cooperation agreements.

In addition to the general requirements for all the countries of the Western Balkans concerning 'respect for democratic principles and the rule of law, and for human rights and fundamental freedoms', the regional approach also incorporated certain country-specific demands.[21] No direct references were made to minority rights per se within the country-specific conditions though the need to address majority-minority relations was clearly implied. In relation to Croatia, compliance with the obligations of Erdut and cooperation with UNTAES and OSCE which would necessarily have a minorities component were stipulated; as regards Bosnia-Herzegovina, the establishment of functioning institutions as provided for in the constitution was broadly specified; and in terms of FRY 'credible pressure on the Bosnian Serbs to cooperate in the institution building and the implementation of provisions of the constitution' as well as evidence that FRY is cooperating with ICTY and the granting of a 'large degree of autonomy' to Kosovo were itemised.[22] Moreover in the annex of elements for examination of compliance, there was a specific section on 'respect for and protection of minorities' which stipulated (i) the right to establish and maintain their own educational, cultural and religious institutions, organisations or associations; (ii) adequate opportunities for these minorities to use their own languages before the courts and public authorities; and (iii) adequate protection of refugees and displaced persons returning to area where they represent an ethnic minority.[23] However as the regional approach was incorporated into the SAP, the actual place of minority rights in the overall Stabilisation and Association process was to become even less apparent.

[21] See Calic, 2005, 4.

[22] Only limited funding was released to Bosnia and directed towards projects in support of the peace agreement rather than to democratic reforms.

[23] See Council conclusions on the principle of conditionality governing the development of the EU's relations with certain countries of south east Europe, http://europa.eu/bulletin/en/9704/p202001.htm.

3. The incremental transformational approach to post-conflict stabilisation and EU integration

With the approval of UN Security Council Resolution 1244 bringing an end to the violence in Kosovo and the aerial bombardment of Serbia by NATO, the broader international community appeared committed to pursuing a comprehensive regional approach to the stabilisation of the Western Balkan region. The Stability Pact which was signed into being in June 1999 was an integral part of the shift from reactive crisis membership to the emergence of a long-term incremental transformational approach to the entire Western Balkan region. With the EU taking the lead, the SP brought together more than 40 countries as well as a range of international organisations in an intergovernmental body to coordinate technical and financial assistance with the objective of facilitating the political stabilisation of the region by fostering 'peace, democracy, respect for human rights and economic prosperity'.[24] The Balkan region was to be stabilised by means of a dual-pronged approach to fostering broader integration with Western economic and security structures as well as renewing and developing regional integration through economic cooperation and a major a programme of reconstruction.[25] Further down the road EU accession would be attainable through the newly established Stabilisation and Association Process.[26]

---

[24] See the SCSP Constituent Document, http://www.stabilitypact.org/constituent/990610-cologne.asp [Accessed January 12, 2008].

[25] The beneficiary states were Albania, Bosnia-Herzegovina, Bulgaria, Croatia, FYROM, Romania and after 2000, Yugoslavia, and June 2001, Moldova,; the neighbouring countries of Hungary, Slovenia and Turkey; members of the EU; non-EU members of the G8, the U.S., Russia, Canada and Japan as well as broad range of international organizations including the EU and European Commission, the UN, OSCE, Council of Europe, UNHCR, NATO and OECD; international financial institutions (IFIs) such as the IMF, World Bank, EIB, EBRD and Council of Europe Development Bank; and regional organisations such as the Black Sea Economic Cooperation, the Central European Initiative, Southeast European Cooperation Initiative (SECI) and the Southeast European Cooperation Process (SEECP). See Phinnemore and Siani-Davies, 2003, 175.

[26] The Pact was built around a South Eastern Europe Regional Table chaired by a Special Coordinator with three working tables on democratisation and human rights, on economic reconstruction, development and cooperation, and security issues. A number of task forces were also attached to the Working Tables exploring human rights and minorities, good governance, media, education and youth, parliamentary cooperation, gender and trafficking in human beings.

In a 2002 policy document the Special Coordinator Edward Busek specified the three principles underlying the approach of the Stability Pact: (i) Western integration in particular with EU accession instruments; (ii) regional cooperation and (iii) regional ownership of the stabilisation process.[27] However, though a sizeable commitment in funds was made at the inauguration of the Stability Pact and a range of regional initiatives with varying degrees of success have been undertaken in the course of its existence, the overall performance of the Pact was hindered by delays in the disbursement of funds, continued political instability in the region, fears or regionalism superseding European integration and also a lack of regional ownership of the stabilisation process.[28] Moreover the EU's primary focus soon became its own Stabilisation and Association Process and tensions emerged between the emphasis on the regional approach and the emerging relationships between Brussels and the countries of the region conditioned as they were around bilateral contractual ties. In 2008 the SP was transformed into the regionally owned Regional Cooperation Council (RCC). However it remains to be seen whether this new institution will provide a firmer basis for a regional cooperation framework in the region.[29]

---

[27] See discussion in Phinnemore and Siani-Davies, 2003.

[28] Spyros Economides, 2001.

[29] Stability Pact, "New milestone set in the Establishment of the Stability Pact Successor – Race Now Open for the Secretary General," Press release, 2 March 2007, available at *http://www.stabilitypact.org/pages/Press/detail.asp?y=2007&p=534.[accessed* on January 22, 2008].

Table 5. 1 The Initiation of the Stabilisation and Association Process

Stabilisation and Association Agreements	
Albania	Negotiations started in 2003 and SAA was signed in 2006
Croatia	SAA signed in 2001 and fully implemented by April 2004. Formal accession negotiations commenced in October 2005. Croatia has made good progress in meeting accession requirements but continues to be berated for its efforts in the field of minority rights, refugee returns, judicial reform and regional cooperation.
Macedonia:	SAA signed in 2001 and fully implemented by February 2005. Macedonia was accepted as an official candidate in November 2005 but has yet to open accession negotiations.
Kosovo:	The Stabilisation Association Tracking Mechanism was established in November 2002 to enable Kosovo to benefit from the SAP. Kosovo was not in position to enter into contractual relations with EU due to its unresolved status. Kosovo declared unilateral independence on February 17, 2008. Its status remains in limbo due to opposition to its independence on the part of Serbia and Russia. EULEX has been set up to manage the process of status settlement but there have been delays in the handover from UNMIK to EULEX.
Bosnia-Herzegovina	Talks on SAA opened in November 2005 and finally concluded in December 2007 thanks to last minute agreement on the integration of police forces. SAA not yet signed.
Serbia	Though the Commission concluded in its Feasibility report of 2005 that Serbia and Montenegro was ready to negotiate a SAA, it was not until April 2008 that the agreement was finally signed and then immediately frozen pending further cooperation with ICTY.
Montenegro	SAA initialled in October 2007, signed in early 2008 and will enter into force following ratification. [[http://ec.europa.eu/enlargement/countries/index_en .htm]]

Following the election of more democratic-oriented governments and the departures of Franjo Tudjman and Slobodan Milosevic in Croatia and the Federal Republic of Yugoslavia respectively, the European Commission building on its Regional Approach formally introduced the 'new' Stabilisation and Association Process (SAP) in 2000 though the organisation and components of the SAP were to be clarified over the following three years. The SAP and the resulting Stabilisation and Association agreements which were to embrace Albania, Bosnia-Herzegovina, Croatia, the FYROM, and Serbia and Montenegro were considered the institutional contribution of the EU to the Stability Pact. They were the culmination of the shift from reactive crisis management to a long-term incremental stabilisation and transformation approach to the Western Balkan region.

Influenced by the experience of the accession process in Central and Eastern Europe, the SAP was at the same time a more comprehensive development framework for the Western Balkans, attempting to take into account the after-effects of conflict and the reverse modernisation experienced by the region, and aiming to promote political stabilisation, marketisation, regional cooperation and potential EU accession. As its name suggests the dual but related processes of stabilisation and association supposedly lie at the heart of the SAP. While the process of association has been markedly shaped by the previous CEEC enlargement rounds, the EU has also sought to tailor this instrument to the conditions of the post-violent conflict states of the Balkans. Yet it is not entirely clear what the EU's definition and objectives are in terms of stabilisation, let alone the exact relationship of stabilisation to association. A careful reading of EU documentation would suggest that stabilisation under SAP refers to a rather broad conceptualisation of regional, political stabilisation embracing a range of elements including compliance with peace agreements, reconstruction and reconciliation, refugee return, cooperation with ICTY and regional cooperation.[30] Cards and later SAP reports also introduced the notion of 'democratic stabilisation' to refer to activities subsumed under refugee return, civil society development and media reform. The lack of clearly formulated benchmarks for stabilisation, however, suggest that it may suffer from the same problems of measurement, moving targets and the risk of politicised judgments that have beset other aspects of EU conditionality in this and other association

[30] See Thessaloniki Agenda 2003 and other SAP Progress Reports.

processes.[31] I will return to the problematic of the application of conditionality later in the chapter.[32]

The SAP is made up of six different elements:

1. Conclusion of new Stabilisation and Association Agreements (SAAs).
2. Development of existing economic and trade relations with and within the region.
3. Development and a partial redirection of existing economic and financial assistance.
4. Assistance for democratisation, civil society, education and institution-building
5. Cooperation in the areas of justice and home affairs
6. Development of political dialogue, including at a multilateral and regional level

It is striking that though the original Communication from the Commission on the Stabilisation and Association process for the countries of South-Eastern Europe acknowledged the importance of human and minority rights as among the primary objectives of the Regional Approach, there was no further mention of this dimension in its early exposition of the six main components of the SAP let alone in the country specific conclusions.[33] This despite the evident relevance of minority rights to a number of the components listed above, and the fact that respect for and protection of minorities are an integral element of the Copenhagen political conditionality. Moreover in the context of the stabilisation and association of the Western Balkan countries, it is clear that policy approaches to minority rights would critically shape future peace-building and democratic consolidation efforts.

The institutionalisation of the SAP marked the beginning of the downgrading of the regional approach in favour of the bilateral mode of interaction. In 'the Western Balkan countries on the road to the European Union' (May 1999) which laid out the rationale behind the SAP, the Commission (i) acknowledged that the prospect of EU membership based on conditionality could serve as a strong driver of reform in the region; (ii) it stressed the need for establishing bilateral relationships among the

[31] European Commission, 2005 Enlargement Strategy, 10. These will be discussed in greater depth later in the chapter.

[32] See Thessaloniki Agenda 2003.

[33] Communication from the Commission to the Council and European Parliament on the Stabilisation and Association process for countries of South Eastern Europe, COM (1999) 235 final, Brussels May 26 1999. Available at: http://aei.pitt.edu/3571/ [accessed January 12, 2008]

countries of the region and (iii) outlined the development of a flexible country-by-country approach based on assistance programmes and contractual relations which would embrace the whole gamut of issues ranging from conflict reconstruction and stabilisation to technical assistance with approximation of legislation.[34]

In June 2000 in Feira the European Council meeting extended its commitment to the SAP countries by offering the prospect of EU membership for the first time and an attendant strategy of support and EU approximation was adopted. The Council Conclusions stated 'The European Council confirms that its objective remains the fullest possible integration of the countries of the region into the political and economic mainstream of Europe...All the countries concerned are potential candidates for EU membership.' [35] At the same time at the Zagreb summit in November 2000, the EU reaffirmed its commitment to supporting the consolidation of democracy and the process of reconciliation and cooperation between the countries of the region.'[36] However as the operationalisation of its policy approach to the Western Balkans evolved and the accent gradually shifted from stabilisation to association, the initial top-down focus on peace-building and regional political stabilisation in the Western Balkans has increasingly been superseded by the top-down drive to meet the requisites of EU membership conditionality. Moreover the EU's regional focus has been displaced in practice in favour of the traditional Brussels-individual country bilateral mode of interaction.

---

[34] The Western Balkan countries on the road to the European Union,' Europe online, available at: http://ec.europa.eu/enlargement/enlargement_process/accession_process/how_does_a_country_join_the_eu/SAP/history_en.htm [accessed on October 12, 2007]

[35] See European Council Santa Maria Da Feira, Presidency Conclusions, 19 and 20 June, 2000, available at: http://www.consilium.europa.eu/ueDocs/cms_Data/docs/pressdata/en/ec/00200-r1.en0.htm [accessed on January 12, 2008]

[36] See Zagreb Summit, final declaration, 24 November 2000 available at: http://ec.europa.eu/enlargement/enlargement_process/accession_process/how_does_a_country_join_the_eu/SAP/zagreb_summit_en.htm [accessed on November 5, 2007]

4. The evolution of the multiple stages of SAP conditionality: the perennial 'moving target' problem

The arrangement of a Stabilisation and Accession Agreement by each of the countries of South Eastern Europe was the focal point of the SAP, which over the long term would lead to formal integration into the EU via the route of candidate status and the subsequent commencement of formal accession negotiations. But the countries of the Western Balkans could not automatically sign SAA agreements.[37] This in itself was a multi-stage process of setting and meeting conditions. The first stage of the conditionality for the participating SAP countries comprised the common principles outlined in the 1996 Regional Approach and the conditionality criteria laid out at the 1997 Council which also included individualised country conditions (discussed above). Respecting these criteria was considered the foundation for the development of bilateral relations with the EC in the field of trade, assistance and contractual relations. As the European Conclusions stated: 'The new process will be based on the existing Regional Approach and reaffirms the European Union's resolve to take up the challenge and responsibility to contribute to stability of the region.'[38] Stabilisation and Association Agreements could only be negotiated after the conditions set out by the European Council in April 1997 on establishing contractual relations as well as the stipulations in the individualised country approaches had been met. In addition the Commission conducts a feasibility study to assess whether the country in question has 'progressed sufficiently to negotiate and meaningfully implement an SAA'. Negotiations over Stabilisation and Association Agreement usually last a year; once signed the agreement needs to be ratified by all EU members and the associated country.

Between 2000 and 2003 additional conditions were incorporated into the SAP framework; in certain cases this included an extension of the conditionality, in others a more precise specification of already stated conditions. The final declaration of the Zagreb Summit of November 2000 emphasised the stage between the signing of the agreements and the opening of formal accession negotiations. It stated that before

[37] For details see EC, Enlargement Strategy, 2005, 9-10.

[38] Council Conclusions on 'The Development of a Comprehensive Policy Based on the Commission Communication On 'The Stabilisation and Association Process For Countries of South-Eastern Europe,' Brussels, 21 June 1999 [available at http://www.consilium.europa.eu/ueDocs/cms_Data/docs/pressdata/en/gena/09008.EN9.htm]

commencing membership negotiations, SAP countries had to respect the criteria defined the Copenhagen Council in June 1993 as well as implement the Stabilisation and Association Agreements. The Copenhagen criteria involved (i) the democratic political criteria, an integral element of which was the minority rights component; (ii) a functioning market economy and the ability to withstand competitive pressures and market forces; and (iii) the ability to take on the obligations of the extensive *acquis communautaire.*[39] In addition to these three primary criteria, Copenhagen 1993 also included a fourth condition for 'entry, the EU's so-called 'let-out clause': 'The Union's capacity to absorb new members while maintaining the momentum of European Integration'. This latter condition was to take on an increasing importance due in part to the slow progress of transformation in the Western Balkans as well as a number of internal EU constraints.

While SAP originally relied mainly on the Phare and Obnova funding mechanisms, a new financial instrument, the Community Assistance for Reconstruction, Development and Stabilisation or Cards was also introduced at Zagreb in November 2000. Cards combined financial assistance directed towards the implementation of the obligations contained in the SAAs with a particular emphasis on institution-building along with asymmetric trade preferences in a bid to facilitate the establishment of a free trade area between the EU and the SAP countries. Cards committed itself to proffering 4.65 billion euros in assistance for the 2000-2006 period. Conditionality was written into the granting and disbursement of funds at three levels: (i) at the level of the objectives of SAP (ii) at the programme level and (iii) at the project level.[40] Moreover, the organisation and management of Cards remained overwhelmingly a centralised Brussels affair with most of the funding directed towards projects drawn up jointly by the Commission and national governments and only a fifth paid directly to national governments for domestic implementation. The Council left itself the ultimate decision-making power to freeze assistance in the case of failure to meet the principles of

[39] See European Council (1993) Presidency Conclusions para. 7 (iii) Copenhagen European Council, 21-22 June. [Available at: http://europa.eu/european_council/conclusions/index_en.htm. Also Grabbe, 2006.

[40] See Zagreb Summit, final declaration, http://ec.europa.eu/enlargement/enlargement_process/accession_process/how_does_a_country_join_the_eu/sap/zagreb_summit_en.htm [accessed on November 12, 2007].

the conditionality.[41] As the Council Conclusions at Zagreb stated 'Where SAP conditionality is not respected, assistance may be frozen'[42]

At the Thessaloniki summit in June 2003 the Council further reinforced the prospect of association and potential membership of the Union by introducing the new instrument of the European Partnership. The strategy was to draw on the instruments used in the CEE accession process to facilitate adjustment to European standards by identifying reform priorities and guiding each country on the steps that need to be taken.[43] European Partnerships lay out the short-term and medium-term priorities for each country as well as commitments against which progress was to be measured. In line with the priorities which have been identified SAP countries are expected to draw up National Plans outlining their fulfilment strategies. According to Pippan the contractual agreements drew heavily on the Europe Agreements with the CEECs though there is also the added emphasis on regional cooperation.[44] Progress was to be monitored in regular annual reports produced for all countries that are part of the SAP whether they have concluded SAAs or not. The additional instrument of political dialogue smacked of earlier experiences of acculturating the Central and Eastern Europeans to EU norms through the Structured Dialogue Process. Likewise the instruments of twinning and TAIEX technical assistance were also made available to SAP countries.

Once the SAA has been implemented, the country is in a position to apply for candidacy status, opening the way for accession negotiations though in contrast to the CEEC accession process, significant time lags can emerge between signing a SAA and being designated a candidate as well as between being designated a candidate and commencing the negotiations process with additional monitoring stages, though not always clear benchmarks, along the way. Macedonia is a good case in point, having signed its SAA in 2001, being designated a candidate in November 2005 but yet to start formal accession negotiations. According to the European Commission 2005 Enlargement Strategy document, the country needs to reach 'a sufficient degree of general compliance with the

---

41 Vachudova, 2003, 152.

42 See Zagreb Summit, final declaration, 24 November 2000, http://ec.europa.eu/enlargement/enlargement_process/accession_process/how_does_a_country_join_the_eu/sap/zagreb_summit_en.htm [accessed on October 13, 2007].

43 European Council, Thessaloniki, Presidency Conclusions, 2003, http://ec.europa.eu/enlargement/key_documents/sap_en.htm [accessed January 11, 2008]

44 See Pippan, 2004.

Copenhagen criteria'. Ultimately the power asymmetry between the countries of the region and Brussels has remained firmly in place. The fact that Brussels retains the political upper hand was also acknowledged in the 2005 EC Enlargement Strategy, which states 'The European Council decides whether and when negotiations can be opened, based on a recommendation from the Commission'.[45]

Croatia signed its SAA in 2001, proceeding to candidate status in June 2004 and opening negotiations a year later in October 2005. Macedonia as indicated above also signed in 2001, had fully implemented its SAA by February 2005 and proceeded to candidate status in November 2005 but has yet to start formal accession negotiations. However, it was not until at least five years later that other countries in the region reached agreement on their SAAs -- Montenegro signed in October 2007 and in the case of both Bosnia-Herzegovina and Serbia, SAAs were initialled but not signed in late 2007. Thus in effect through the instrument of the SAP additional formal layers of conditionality were introduced into the accession process, building on the path followed by the CEECs (shaped as it was by adjustment to the Copenhagen criteria and to European Standards) but at the same time creating a prolonged, multi-phase process during which conditionality could be leveraged upon the countries of the region. While prolonging the period during which the countries of the region were in throes to the conditionality demands of the EU was arguably an appropriate approach for the under-developed post-conflict countries of the Western Balkans, this threatened to further exacerbate the moving target problem identified by Hughes, Sasse and Gordon.[46]

The instrument of the SAP has been refined over time – arguably refined and drawn out – for a number of reasons relating both to developments in the different countries of the WB region as well as intra-EU factors as well. Not only has the Commission undergone a learning curve itself about the political and economic situation in the countries of the Western Balkans as well as deriving lessons from the CEECs enlargement process in particular with regard to Bulgaria and Romania, this has also been coupled with the apparent slow progress in terms of both stabilisation and adjustment in the SAP countries themselves, reflected in the Commission's annual progress reports. Progress has also been slowed by growing divisions in the European Council about how far the EU should enlarge, the perceived tensions between widening versus deepening

---

[45] European Commission, 2005 Enlargement Strategy Paper, 10. See http://eur-lex.europa.eu/smartapi/cgi/sga_doc?smartapi!celexplus!prod!CELEXnumdoc&lg=en&numdoc=505DC0561 [accessed on January 13, 2008]

[46] Hughes, Sasse and Gordon, 2004.

both of which have contributed to so-called 'enlargement fatigue' inside certain quarters of the EU itself as well as in certain member states. Moreover along with the perennial concern about candidates' administrative capacities, increasing weight has been attached to the rather vague notion of 'absorption capacity', the fourth condition of Copenhagen 1993 with a proposal tabled (though rejected) at the European Council in June 2006 by France, Austria and the Netherlands for it to be made a formal part of the accession conditionality criteria.[47] Clearly the credibility of conditionality as an instrument will be further watered down if decisions about the progress of candidates and potential candidates are to be shaped by judgements about intra-EU capacities over which potential members have no influence.

5. SAP as a modified template of CEE Accession Process

The SAP as suggested above was strongly influenced by the evolution of the instruments of the accession process in nearby post-communist CEE. Of course the fundamental difference between these two regions was that the CEECs in contrast to the Western Balkans experienced a different degree of ethnicisation of politics and varying state- and nation-building challenges in the wake of communist collapse. Moreover the CEECs did not have to find ways to accommodate complex majority-minority relations within states as well as across former federal structures in the wake of the massive disruption, dislocation and devastation wrought by war. This factor inevitably raises the question of the appropriateness of a template largely developed for a set of countries in rather different circumstances and then modified -- more considerably in rhetoric than in practice -- to fit the current situation in the countries of the Western Balkans which on the whole continue to be characterised by weak state institutions, economic backwardness and ethnic tensions.

The EU did undertake efforts to galvanise attention on regional stabilisation in response to the post-conflict situation. In line with this a set of policies, areas of cooperation and putative regional agreements were outlined as part of the Final Declaration at Zagreb to reinforce the EU's 1997 Regional Approach in areas ranging from political dialogue, the establishment of a free trade area, cooperation in justice and home affairs.

---

47 Michael Emerson, Senem Aydin, Julia De Clerck-Sachsse and Gergana Noutcheva, 'Just what is this 'absorption capacity' of the European Union?', CEPS Policy Brief, October 2006, available at:
http://shop.ceps.eu/BookDetail.php?item_id=1381

The final declaration even stated: 'Rapprochement with the European Union will go hand in hand with this process of developing regional cooperation.'[48] But in reality this latter component of the SAP has not lived up to the lofty but perhaps unrealistic expectation that regionalism and European integration would complement each other. The overwhelmingly bilateral basis of the SAP – in terms of the SAA agreement negotiations and the annual reporting process, the centralised vertical organisation of the funding instruments, and the drive for EU integration which superseded and in the eyes of the national governments worked against regional cooperation -- have all militated against the furthering of the regional approach. In fact where regional integration has taken place beyond improvement of trade relations among the former states of Yugoslavia, this has been the result of European-level projects rather than a regional affair.[49]

Compared to the accession roadmap for the CEECs, the SAAs constituted a new multi-layered interim step with additional conditioning options along the road to membership. Though the full commitment to membership was laid on the table upfront (earlier on in comparison with the CEECs' enlargement process), the EU appeared at the same time to be prolonging the overall process leaving additional leeway in the hands of the Commission. In SAP a new category of 'potential membership' was introduced which still holds out the promise of eventual membership but lengthens even further the ill-defined time-frames involved – leaving additional leeway in the hands of the Commission. As the 2005 Enlargement Strategy Paper acknowledged: 'The accession negotiations can last for widely varying numbers of years, depending on the country. By their very nature, negotiations are an open-ended process.'[50]

As the framework and organisation of SAP has evolved since its inception in 2000, it has become increasingly apparent with the gradual broadening of the stages of conditionality, that in practice many of the problems and shortcomings identified by Hughes, Sasse and Gordon in their analysis of conditionality in the CEECs accession process -- in particular the inherent fluidity of the conditionality and the consequent 'moving target problem' as a result of unclear benchmarking procedures,

---

[48] Ibid.

[49] M. Uvalic, 2001. Uvalic has shown that there has been only limited economic integration with other countries in broader Balkan region. See also Phinnemore and Siani-Davies, 2003, 181.

[50] European Commission, 2005 Enlargement Strategy Paper, 10. ee http://eur-lex.europa.eu/smartapi/cgi/sga_doc?smartapi!celexplus!prod!CELEXnumdoc&lg=en&numdoc=505DC0561 [accessed on January 13, 2008]

imprecise measurements of progress and the predominance of politically-influenced decision procedures and accompanying loss of credibility – have been magnified in the Western Balkans given the complex range of domestic post-conflict settlement political issues the countries of the region face. Internal divisions among member states about future enlargements and the future borders of the EU and increasingly voiced concerns about the vaguely formulated 'absorption capacity' run the risk of further diluting the instrument of conditionality.

The overwhelming focus on a top-down approach to the organisation of SAP, the concentration on national elites and the centralised fund management approach may have appeared in the short-term to have been the most appropriate approach given the limited technical, infrastructural and human capacities even at the central level in the Western Balkans. But this approach is likely to store up greater problems and potentially contribute to further societal breakdown in the future in post-conflict societies where ethnic divides remain strong and sub-national elites need to be co-opted into the political and socio-economic process of domestic reconstruction and transition, and EU integration. The top-down imposition of policies from outside and the primary concentration on preparing for meeting EU-acquis related requirements may not be the most appropriate approach to post-war societies where a different set of priorities (including funding priorities) may deliver more effective outcomes over the long term – including more carefully targeted policies at all levels to develop domestic governance structures, to cultivate conflict management and reconciliation capacities and to foster domestic and regional ownership.[51]

6. Minority Rights and Post-Conflict Stabilisation

This section explores the relationship in SAP between the EU accession process, minority issues and post-conflict stabilisation. Through its focus on minority rights it questions how far the SAP constitutes an effective approach tailored to the conditions of the post-(violent) conflict Western Balkans taking into account the particular political and socio-economic needs generated by the complex majority-minority relations in the post-warring countries or rather whether it is more proximate to an amended CEEC enlargement approach which insufficiently addresses the specific needs of the region. It explores what the notion of minority rights

[51] See discussion in Roberto Belloni, 2007, 20.

as a key component of reconciliation has meant both in rhetoric and practice in EU policy documents and funding instruments as well as seeking to understand the operation of conditionality in this area.

It is argued here that that though the EU's approach to minority rights has evolved since the inception of SAP in 2000, the EU does not have a fully conceptualised approach to minority rights at the domestic or regional level. Initially considerable concentration was placed on narrow conceptions of refugee return and property rights. Attention was also given to delivering justice through the instrument of ICTY. Over time the need to establish appropriate legal frameworks has been increasingly prioritised. Socio-economic and cultural issues have also emerged as areas of concern in recent years. Secondly it is suggested that in practice both in terms of policy delivery and implementation mechanisms, the EU has ended up relying on a trickle-down approach to conflict resolution and majority-minority reconciliation based on anticipated peace dividends from economic and social stabilisation with some fragments of more targeted conflict management policies in the area of minority rights protection. Contrary to its objectives the SAP process has to date proved inadequate in facilitating post-conflict reconciliation at the sub-national and local levels and may in the long term given the considerable socio-economic and political disparities among different communities in different regions spur future instability.

From the commencement of the Stabilisation and Association Process, the EU presented rapprochement with the EU and democratic consolidation and regional reconciliation and cooperation as two sides of the same coin. In the Zagreb summit final declaration in June 2000 the EU affirmed that 'democracy and regional reconciliation and cooperation on the one hand, and the rapprochement of each of these countries with the European Union on the other, form a whole'.[52] However despite the central place ascribed to minority rights protection as part of the conditionality framework, SAP has largely failed to deliver an integrated approach to reconciliation in the area of minority rights. Rather it has constituted a replication of the pre-CEE accession process with certain additional elements appended on in an attempt to address the particular specificities of the Western Balkans region (including refugee return, cooperation with ICTY and national legal frameworks). In addition to the Copenhagen criteria, which framed the Enlargement Strategy in CEE, the

---

[52] See Zagreb Summit, final declaration, 24 November 2000, http://ec.europa.eu/enlargement/enlargement_process/accession_process/how_does_a_country_join_the_eu/sap/zagreb_summit_en.htm [accessed on November 12, 2007].

SAP added a set of conditions specific to the situation in the Western Balkans. These conditions, as indicated above, were laid out for the first time in the Council Conclusions of 29 April 1997 and became the conditionality basis for SAP at the Zagreb summit in November 2000. In addition to the implementation of market-oriented and democratising reforms which also applied to Central and Eastern Europe during the enlargement process, the 1997 Council conclusions included four sets of conditions specific to the Western Balkans: (1) human rights and minority protection; (2) progress on refugee return, (3) cooperation with ICTY and (4) good neighbourliness and compliance with international/regional obligations (including peace agreements).[53] Regarding the protection of minority rights, the 1997 Council Conclusion included: (1) the right of minorities to create and maintain educational, cultural and religious institutions, organisations or associations; (2) the provision of reasonable possibilities for minorities to use their language before tribunals and public authorities; (3) the adequate protection of refugees and displaced persons returning to the region whether they constitute an ethnic minority.[54]

This Thessaloniki Agenda fleshed out SAP's approach to minority issues further: the main focus remained on refugee return. Some emphasis was also placed on the enactment and implementation of legal frameworks for refugee return and anti-discrimination legislation for minorities. Finally Thessaloniki in rhetoric at least also laid stress on cultural and socio-economic issues including actions in the areas of education, media, civil society and employment as well as respect for religious, cultural and linguistic diversity.[55] As the Summit Declaration stated, 'The EU will continue to work closely with the Western Balkan countries to further consolidate peace and promote stability, democracy, the rule of law, and respect for human and minority rights. Inviolability of international borders, peaceful resolution of conflicts and regional cooperation are principles of highest importance.' The Council went on to reiterate its support for the full implementation of UN Security Council Resolution

---

[53] Council conclusions on the principle of conditionality governing the development of the European Union's relations with certain countries of south-east Europe', 29 April 1997, http://europa.eu/bulletin/en/9704/p202001.htm [accessed November 12, 2007]

[54] Ibid.

[55] The Thessaloniki Agenda for the Western Balkans, 16 June 2003, http://ec.europa.eu/enlargement/enlargement_process/accession_process/how_does_a_country_join_the_eu/sap/thessaloniki_agenda_en.htm [accessed January 13, 2008]

1244, Dayton, Ohrid and Belgrade; to stress the imperative of full cooperation with ICTY and also to promote further return of refugees and IDPs. [56]

Though SAP documentation has always stressed the importance of the regional dimension, the linkage to minority rights as an important aspect of ethnic reconciliation in this context has been more indirect and diffuse. The focus in practice has rather tended to be the establishment of trade relations, cooperation in energy and border management, etc. In terms of minority rights, it is suggested here that in the framework of SAP, refugee return has formed the primary area of action within human rights and the protection of minorities with a secondary focus on establishing appropriate legal frameworks in line with the Council of Europe Framework Convention on National Minorities. This is not only apparent in Council conclusions and other declaratory statements but is also evidenced through an analysis of actual fund allocations which takes us beyond the stage of priority-setting. (See below) The Thessaloniki Summit Declaration outlined the following policy approaches for refugee return in reasonable detail: (i) the enactment and enforcement of anti-discrimination legislation ensuring fair and proportionate representation of minorities in employment, particularly in public institutions; (ii) provision of adequate security conditions, non-discriminatory education and all other basic services; (iii) resolution of outstanding property issues; (iv) provision for monitoring of initiatives concerning return and reintegration.[57] The overriding priority of refugee return as the main line of approach to post-conflict minority issues is also in the Cards 2002-6 Regional Strategy Paper which states 'Of all the problems facing minorities in the region, the situation on the war-displaced is the most significant.'[58] The approach is further justified in the context of the experience of ethnic cleansing: 'This national focus in helping refugees return is not only a practical necessity, it is also correct that a country which created conditions for ethnic cleansing in the past must face its responsibilities by correcting and reversing such conditions.'[59]

---

[56] Thessaloniki Summit Declaration, http://www.consilium.europa.eu/ueDocs/cms_Data/docs/pressdata/en/gena/76201.pdf [accessed December 27, 2007]

[57] Ibid.

[58] CARDS assistance to the Western Balkans: Regional Strategy Paper, 2002-2006, European Commission, 2002, http://www.reliefweb.int/library/documents/2001/ec_balkans_22oct.pdf [accessed December 27, 2007], 10.

[59] Ibid.

Though the EU has in other statements made reference to ethnic reconciliation and minority rights under different terms, these statements have not been backed up with specific benchmarking and enforcement tools. The Thessaloniki summit asserted that 'the EU places high priority on initiatives and activities aiming at reconciling for the future, through overcoming legacies of the past, which are obstacles to normalisation and democratic development. In this respect, the role of education, social development and culture is essential in changing mentalities, promoting tolerance, ensuring ethnic and religious coexistence and shaping modern democratic societies.' But it has relied on the work of other organisations to address these issues including UNESCO, Council of Europe, the Stability Pact and SEECP as well as a number of NGOs. The EU has claimed that this is to avoid overlap and maximise resource usage but an alternative explanation would highlight the lack of EU capacity in these areas and the secondary importance that the EU attaches to such issues compared to the hard-nosed realities of refugee and migration flows. Finally while it is true that in the European Partnerships a greater degree of breadth and specificity is injected into the action plans on minority rights for SAP countries, even here the underlying somewhat skewed priority list outlined above remains in place if less pronounced (firstly refugee return, secondly the establishment of legal frameworks including those facilitating refugee return and thirdly socio-economic and cultural concerns). In addition the whole process is beset by the problem of unclear benchmarking and a lack of clear criteria for the priorities identified to which I now turn.

7. The challenge of operationalising minority rights conditionality

In its rhetoric and a number of its legal and policy instruments, the EU subscribes to the norm of minority rights protection. It also attaches significance to the role of minority rights in its relations with external countries, in particular those attempting to accede to the Union. Moreover as indicated above 'respect for and protection of minorities' is clearly laid out as part of the political Copenhagen criterion for opening membership negotiations with the EU.[60] Furthermore as part of the process of

---

[60] European Council (1993) Presidency Conclusions para. 7 (iii) Copenhagen European Council, 21-22 June. [Available at: http://europa.eu/european_council/conclusions/index_en.htm]

monitoring compliance for candidate and potential candidate SAP countries, the EU in its annual reporting process seeks to evaluate the position of and progress on minority rights. The problem, as Sasse has pointed out in her writings on the place of the EU in minority protection, is that the (i) 'minority condition' lacks a firm foundation in EU law (ii) there is a lack of appropriate instruments which directly translate into the *acquis communautaire* to enable minority rights' monitoring and protection, let alone concise benchmarks for assessing compliance at both the national and sub-national levels.[61] More broadly speaking the question of what constitutes a minority and the nature of minority rights remains a matter of dispute in international law.[62] This situation which Sasse characterised as having contributed to a case of 'normative overstretch' in relation to the CEEC accessions is equally if not more problematic when it comes to the operationalisation of EU conditionality, the credibility of conditions and the ability of EU to induce compliance in the post-warring countries of the Western Balkans.[63]

Despite the very different history of majority-minority relations in post-communist Central and Eastern Europe and problems in the operationalisation of minority conditionality during their accession process, the EU's approach towards the protection of minorities in the Western Balkans has been similarly devised and implemented. Though SAP introduced a new area of action within the criterion of human rights and minority protection, namely that of refugee return, few changes have been made from the previous enlargement round in the area of benchmarks, standards and operationalisation. Unlike in the CEECs accession round whereby the first Copenhagen criterion had supposedly to be fulfilled by the time accession negotiations were commenced, the new instrument of the SAAs under the SAP should in principle mean that the EU has greater political leverage to facilitate the strengthening of minority rights protection than in the previous enlargement rounds.

Two clear areas of weakness can be highlighted in the SAP's approach towards minority protection in the Western Balkans. Firstly, the SAP fails to adequately tackle the distinctive nature of the problems of minorities in the Western Balkans. Even if the EU has acknowledged some of the challenges facing the countries of the Western Balkans in relation to national minorities and inter-ethnic reconciliation (in both

[61] The EU relies on other regional and international norms rather than its own standards. The Framework Convention for the Protection of National Minorities continues to be the reference framework for the Western Balkans.

[62] Sasse, 2005, 5 and Hughes and Sasse, 2003, 12-13.

[63] Sasse, 2005. See also discussion in Tocci, 2007, 25 and 177.

Council statements and also in progress reports) the enlargement machinery has tended to reproduce itself in this area. Secondly, inherent problems remain as suggested above with the definition and implementation of a policy towards national minorities.[64] A closer examination of the progress reports, European partnerships and evolving EU enlargement strategy papers reveal that despite attention to the establishment of appropriate legal frameworks for the protection and respect of minorities, the EU approach in this area remains beset by a lack of clear benchmarks and standards, difficulties in measuring progress, inherent inconsistencies, ill-targeted activities and a general disregard for differences among the countries of the region as well as at the sub-national level within particular countries.

8. Measuring progress and the lack of clear benchmarks

In terms of the lack of precise standards and benchmarks in certain minority-related issues, the 2007 Enlargement Strategy paper stresses that 'all countries need to encourage a spirit of tolerance towards minorities and take appropriate measures to protect persons who may be subject to discrimination, hostility or violence. This is essential to achieve reconciliation and stability'. Later it states that 'in the area of the protection of minorities further efforts are necessary to combat intolerance and ethnic discrimination, as well as to improve the implementation of legislation concerning minorities'.[65] The individual country progress reports also lay out similarly worthy objectives, but neither the Strategy document nor the country-specific progress reports contain operational tools, specific confidence-building measures or measurable benchmarks with which to address these issues, nor are concomitant financial allocations provided as discussed below. Thus the 2006 and 2005 Croatia Reports both highlight the need for greater tolerance and reconciliation; in the case of the 2005 report, the Commission endorses 'peaceful

---

[64] Sebastian has suggested an additional layer of complexity or fuzziness in that though there is no clear definition of what constitutes a minority in EU law, there appears to be a discrepancy in the case of BiH at least between the concept of a minority and standard for minority protection from the EU's perspective versus the position of the B-H as stated in its law on the protection of rights of national minorities adopted in June 2002 according to which the three constituent peoples are not considered national minorities.

[65] 2007 Enlargement Strategy Paper, 6 [Available at: http://ec.europa.eu/enlargement/key_documents/reports_nov_2007_en.htm]

coexistence', whereas in the 2006 report initiatives promoting 'integration' are encouraged but in neither case is there any specification of benchmarks in this area.[66] Likewise the 2007 Croatia Progress Report states that 'Croatia needs to encourage a spirit of tolerance towards the Serb minority and take appropriate measures to protect those who may still be subject to threats or acts of discrimination, hostility or violence.' The FYROM 2007 Progress report stresses in a similar broad vein 'Further efforts are needed to fully implement the [Ohrid Framework A]greement and to consolidate confidence between the political parties representing the different ethnic communities. A consensual approach and readiness to compromise are necessary and the spirit of the agreement should be more consistently applied.'[67] On the whole the pitch of the writing remains declaratory rather than precise, focused and reflecting targeted responses to the situation on the ground particularly at sub-national levels.

Given the overall absence of clear benchmarks and standards, the Commission is faced with the problem of precisely measuring the progress (or lack thereof) that has been achieved in the SAP countries. This has given rise to inconsistencies in the reporting process and more importantly a resulting loss of credibility in the Commission's work. On the whole the Commission reports developments in rather general, arguably vague terms. Thus the 2007 Progress Report for Croatia acknowledges 'Some progress has been made in the area of human rights and the protection of minorities. Legal provisions on human rights protection are in general adequate but a number of important challenges remain in terms of implementation.'[68]

Not surprisingly refugee return has been more easily quantifiable and thus lends more ,manifestly to measures of progress but even in this area the passage of laws on refugee return and the enumeration of the numbers of returnees tells us little about the actual economic and social reintegration of returnees, the record of which has proved rather problematic. Thus for example, the BiH 2003 Progress Report pointed out that by the end of 2002 'almost one million refugees and displaced persons, among them around 390,000 minority returnees have been able to return home. Estimates put the number of remaining displaced person

---

[66] Reconciliation between ethnic groups is included as an objective for the first time in the 2005 Croatia report. Footnote Croatian reports on EU website

[67] 20007 Progress Report for FYROM [Available at: http://ec.europa.eu/enlargement/key_documents/reports_nov_2007_en.htm]

[68] 2007 Progress Report for Croatia, 31. [Available at: http://ec.europa.eu/enlargement/key_documents/reports_nov_2007_en.htm]

registered in BiH at around 367,000.'[69] The report does acknowledge that minority returnees have faced considerable local socio-economic difficulties and harassment. Similarly the 2003 Croatia Progress Report points to a lack of economic opportunities for returnees as well as continuing tensions in local communities.[70] The 2005 Progress Report reiterates and expands on these problems. 'There are still real obstacles to the sustainable return of Serb refugees, such as enduring hostility in certain localities and remaining housing concerns'. The report also mentions problems in access to employment for Serbs, even those who remained in Croatia during the war. The fact of the continuing lack of progress in terms of socio-economic reintegration of returnees was highlighted again in the 2007 enlargement strategy which acknowledges that no satisfactory progress has been achieved in this area.

A closer look at the case of Bosnia-Herzegovina highlights many of the problems of lack of measurable benchmarks, inconsistencies and flip-flopping as well as the gap between the adoption of legal provisions and implementation discussed above. The 2000 Road Map for BiH laid out a set of broad benchmarks for Bosnia to comply with in the course of 2000 including steps in the field of democracy, human rights and the rule of law, the implementation of property laws as well as a renewed engagement at all levels to create conditions for sustainable returns.[71] Commenting on progress achieved by the country in meeting the steps laid out in the Road Map and SAP, the 2003 BiH Progress Report pointed out that 'BiH prioritized the Road Map, achieving substantial completion in September 2002', though no further specification was included and subsequent comments in the report appear to contradict this basic claim.[72] Thus the report also stated: 'The record on the implementation of Road Map legislation remains moderate. There is little proof that BiH has used

---

[69] 2003 BiH Progress Report.
[Available at:
http://ec.europa.eu/enlargement/bosnia_and_herzegovina/key_documents_en.htm]

[70] 2003 Croatia Progress Report, 20. [Available at:
http://eurlex.europa.eu/smartapi/cgi/sga_doc?smartapi!celexplus!prod!CELEXnumdoc&lg=en&numdoc=503DC0139]

[71] These included the implementation of decisions of the human rights institutions; the approval and implementation of laws on judicial and prosecutorial service in the Federation and the law on court and judicial service in the RS; cooperation with OHR in implementation of public service broadcasting at state and entity level

[72] 2003 BiH Progress Report. [Available at:
http://ec.europa.eu/enlargement/bosnia_and_herzegovina/key_documents_en.htm]

the Road Map and 'EU' requirements to dynamise reform'.[73] Meanwhile only a page later, the report commented 'Clearly SAP and the prospect of a SAA remained a top government priority'. '[T]here is little evidence of a qualitative acceleration of reform.' While certain Road Map points were declared completed, the related legislation frequently remained without practical implementation.

The 2003 Feasibility report encouraged BiH to 'complete outstanding Road Map steps' in the 16 priorities/benchmarks that the EC had identified for action in the course of 2004.[74] The fifth priority identified by the Feasibility study 2003 for BiH concerned 'effective human rights provisions.' The areas of action included: 'Adopt and bring into force outstanding legislation supporting refugee returns. In particular, introduce, adopt and implement legislation on the BiH Refugee Return Fund. Complete the transfer of the human rights bodies to BiH control. Ensure that unresolved cases of the Human Rights Chamber are dealt with and that the Chamber's responsibilities are transferred to the Constitutional Court. Provide adequate funding for the Court. Assume full national responsibility for the State Ombudsman and make progress on the merger of the State and Entity Ombudsmen.' It is surprising that no mention was made of minority issues nor inter-ethnic reconciliation in the BiH 2003 Feasibility Report despite the fact that the continuing problem of ethnic divisions and the basic issue of state dysfunctionality as a result of the ethnic veto mechanisms are acknowledged.[75] For example, the report stresses the 'persistent thinking in ethnic categories.'[76] With respect to the functioning of the Parliamentary assembly in BiH the report points out, 'Members of the State Parliament still often vote along ethnic lines … occasionally leading to blockage.' Even more importantly, the Feasibility report stresses, 'the divisions that were so clearly and tragically demonstrated during the 1992-1993 war have not yet been entirely overcome.'[77] Moreover, progress in these areas was linked to the prospect of concluding a Stabilisation and Association Agreement.[78]

---

[73] Ibid, 20.

[74]http://eurlex.europa.eu/smartapi/cgi/sga_doc?smartapi!celexplus!prod!CELEXnumdoc&lg=en&numdoc=503DC0692 [accessed November 23, 2007]

[75] See Bose, 2002, for discussion of post-Dayton political framework in Bosnia-Herzegovina.

[76] 2003 Feasibility Study on Bosnia, 7.
http://eurlex.europa.eu/smartapi/cgi/sga_doc?smartapi!celexplus!prod!CELEXnumdoc&lg=en&numdoc=503DC0692 [accessed January 13, 2008]

[77] Ibid, 14. The study acknowledged that some slow progress had been made in overcoming ethnic divisions at the institutional level but that little progress had

Two year later in October 2005 the European Commission concluded that BiH had made significant progress in addressing the 16 priority areas identified by the 2003 Feasibility Study, including issuing a reasonably positive report on progress relating to priority no. 5., and therefore recommended the opening of negotiations for SAA.[79] Once again the European Council listed a number of areas on which the authorities should concentrate, but no mention was made of minority issues, or minority issues as a critical part of reconciliation processes. However within a month in 2005 BiH Progress Report though the Commission concluded that progress has been made in the area of human rights, the chapter on human rights and protection of minorities appears to tell a different story, reiterating a familiar set of problematic areas and unresolved issues. In the case of Bosnia, the 2007 Progress Report states 'Little progress has been made in relation to human rights and protection of minorities. Overall implementation of international human rights conventions needs to improve…In the area of protection of minorities further efforts are necessary to combat intolerance and ethnic discrimination as well as to improve the implementation of legislation concerning minorities.'[80] The risk of the loss of credibility among the countries of the region in the EU's monitoring and assessment activities is underlined by the somewhat cynical comments of Zivanovic in his assessment of BiH in the Balkan Yearbook of Human Rights in 2006 where he states 'Just by examining the EU documents in the period 2003 and 2006, it is possible to conclude that the list of human rights issues to be resolved is almost the same. Domestic human rights reports are even more pessimistic. Human rights do not belong to mainstream EU activities related to Bosnia-Herzegovina.'[81]

---

been made in relation to the continuing ethnic divisions at both the political and societal level.

[78] Ibid. 'Dealing with these divisions and securing a functioning state is important in the context of a SAA'.

[79] See http://europa.eu/rapid/pressReleasesAction.do?reference=IP/05/1329&format=HTML&aged=0&language=EN&guiLanguage=en [accessed May 19, 2008].

[80] 2007 Progress Report for Bosnia-Herzegovina, 26. [Available at: http://ec.europa.eu/enlargement/key_documents/reports_nov_2007_en.htm]

[81] Miroslav Zivanovic, 2006, 68.

9. The gap between rhetorical commitments and funding

In addition there appears to be a striking gap between the priorities identified in the European Partnerships and progress reports and the actual funding allocations devoted to minority protection under Cards. A close examination of the Cards funding allocations sheds light on this point. Even if there is variation among countries, overall it can be concluded that though a considerable level of funding has been allocated to political and administrative requirements, in particular good governance, institution-building and capacity building, and especially since 2004, over time as the EU's focus has shifted towards preparation for closer integration and ultimate membership, more funds have been devoted towards meeting EU standards at the expense of issues relating to democratic stabilisation. In the case of reconciliation and minority rights the main focus has been refugee return and to a degree economic reconstruction.

If levels of funding are indicative of the priority attached to a particular issue for the EU, then it can be deduced that minority protection is not a priority area. Under Cards there is not even a separate budget line devoted to minority protection. Minority protection figures as a separate line only for Croatia under Phare 2005-2006. Even so this line only accounted for one percent of total allocations under Phare. In 2005 for example human rights and protection of minorities received only 1.3 million of allocations out of a total of 71.5 million euros (i.e. 0.9 percent). On the whole the protection of minorities is subsumed under the rubric of democratic stabilisation which entails activities in the areas of refugee return and civil society development.[82] In the case of FYROM, 'inter-ethnic relations and civil society' are included under the rubric of 'democracy and rule of law', receiving only 3 million out of more than 40 million each year for the period 2001-2004. In 2005-2006 'democracy and rule of law' was aimed at minority rights but received only 2 million out of the 85 million allocated for this country during the period. Moreover, following the introduction of the Instrument for Pre-Accession Assistance (IPA) for 2007-2013,[83] allocations to minority protection are even more

---

[82] Serbia and Kosovo are exceptions as democratic stabilisation does not figure as a separate line until 2005. Most allocations were directed towards reconstruction and managed by the European Agency for Reconstruction.

[83] Serious concerns about the IPA were raised in a European Stability Initiative report which argued that the two-tier funding proposals threatened to sow further discord among the countries of the Western Balkans – between the candidates and pre-in or potential candidates. Though ESI's criticism was not entirely grounded and the EU's assessment was in part based on the question of the capacities of SAP

difficult to gauge given that funding distribution falls into two main components for potential candidates, i.e. 'transition assistance and institution building' and 'cross border cooperation'. Minority protection and refugee return are subsumed under the first component but the multi-annual indicative planning fails to disaggregate allocations within each component. The priority areas within the first component include activities such as support for civil society, media, public administration, rule of law, judicial system, refugee return and support to minorities and vulnerable groups, etc.

The only minority protection area that has received significant funding under Cards is that of refugee return. Refugee return was the most important allocation under Cards for BiH for the period 2001-2003 though this allocation has decreased significantly since 2003. In Croatia refugee return was never the most important item under Cards but figured prominently together with Economic and Social Development, though there has been a reduction in allocations for refugee return in Croatia since 2005.[84] In the case of FYROM there have been no allocations for refugee return at all. It may be that in the case of BiH and Croatia the reduction in funds for refugee return reflects a shift in approach to the issue of refugees and IDPs – despite shortfalls in progress over refugee return, it may be that the problem of refugees had by then changed into that of ensuring the appropriate socio-economic and political conditions for newly return displaced person, i.e. a 'minority-related issue' of a different kind.[85] In the case of FRY and Kosovo it is also somewhat surprising that there were no financial provisions for refugee return until 2005. In fact most allocations

---

countries to absorb the funds, the ESI report highlighted the potential ambiguities of a vertical integration process with the EU vis-à-vis promoting stabilisation and integration at the regional level. See 'Breaking out of the Balkan Ghetto: Why IPA should be changed', ESI Report, 2005. See http://www.esiweb.org/pdf/esi_document_id_66.pdf [accessed November 22, 2007]

[84] Funding for administrative capacity-building also featured prominently in the case of Croatia, coming third after Economic and Social Development and Refugee Return, highlighting the EU's underlying interest in preparing Croatia's administratively to take on the obligations of the acquis.

[85] On refugee return to Croatia, see OSCE Report 'Background Report on Refugee Return in Croatia and the Status of Implementation of January 2005 Sarajevo Ministerial Declaration on Refugee Return', http://www.osce.org/croatia/documents.html?lsi=true&limit=10&grp=270 [accessed November 22, 2007]. See also section nine http://www.oscebih.org/documents/OSCE10Years.pdf on the Return Programme [accessed November 22, 2007].

under Cards for FRY and Kosovo were devoted to economic reconstruction. The issue of democratic stabilisation was overlooked until 2005 which seems rather late in the day. Even civil society development has received very little EU funding, including through EIDHR.[86] The activities that are included under the rubric of civil society do not address the issue of inter-ethnic cooperation, reconciliation or protection. In fact under Cards no single project is devoted to this area.

SAP conditionality has led to the adoption or strengthening of some minorities legislation in the countries of the Western Balkans and varying levels of funding for some minority rights programmes but there have clearly been gaps and weaknesses in the implementation of minority rights policies at the sub-national level which is reflective of a disconnect between national and sub-national level in terms of the involvement of actors in EU processes and management of instruments. This disconnect is arguably even more serious in post-conflict situation given enduring antagonisms at various levels and the potential negatives consequences of the lack of local ownership as well as continuing divisions between the local, regional and federal levels. Overall despite the priorities listed in the European Partnerships and the often critical assessment of the progress reports on refugee return, an analysis of Cards allocations reveals: (i) a gap between stated priorities and commitments and actual efforts to address the problem of post-conflict ethnic divisions and protection of minorities and (ii) reliance on an implicit trickle-down approach to minority protection and reconciliation (with the possible exception of support for refugee return).

Conclusion

Despite the introduction of new elements in an attempt to address the specific conditions of the post-conflict states of the Western Balkans, the SAP process has in large part resembled a repackaged pre-accession CEEC instrument. Notwithstanding the rhetoric of regionalism and reconciliation, in practice the Commission has chosen to rely on the tried and tested models of bilateralism and conditionality with the promise of accession as the prime incentive structure around which the compliance of the countries in the region was to be secured. The EU's approach to minority rights in the context of reconciliation has remained rather narrow, mainly concentrated on refugee return with a certain attention to building

---

[86] See http://ec.europa.eu/europeaid/projects/eidhr/eidhr_en.htm [accessed November 23, 2007].

legislative frameworks and to cooperation with ICTY and limited attention at best to other socio-economic and cultural issues and to the issue of good neighbourliness. The range of policies aimed at facilitating inter-ethnic cooperation nationally and regionally has been rather narrow and has largely been delivered through a Commission-to-national government level interaction based on centralised administrative management structures which arguably has hampered progress in a number of policy areas throughout the Western Balkan region. As the most recent SAP reports suggest, progress in implementation is at best extremely slow in the countries of the region.[87] As Borzel and Risse acknowledged: 'EU membership has not motivated Balkan leaders very strongly to undertake the necessary reforms as was the case in Central and Eastern Europe where regime transformation had been peaceful.'[88] The importance of ensuring domestic and regional ownership and the building of capacities at sub-national and local levels have been largely overlooked in this process, an issue which marred the CEEC accession process and is likely to have even more significant repercussions for regional stability and majority-minority relations in a post-violent conflict region.

References

EU documents

Conclusions of the General Affairs Council of 26 February 1996 A Regional Approach to the countries of South-Eastern Europe: http://www.consilium.europa.eu/ueDocs/cms_Data/docs/pressdata/en/gena/028a0001.htm

European Commission, Communication from the Commission to the Council and European Parliament on the Stabilisation and Association process for countries of South Eastern Europe, COM (1999) 235 final, Brussels May 26 1999. Available at: http://aei.pitt.edu/3571/ [

—. Cards Assistance to the Western Balkans: Regional Strategy Paper, 2002-2006,

[87] For example, the Croatia 2004 Progress Report acknowledges that the provisions concerning housing solutions to returning refugees and IDPs have not been implemented. Likewise the 2005 Bosnian Progress Report points to problems in the Application of the Framework Convention for National Minorities with regard to the Roma population.

[88] Borzel and Risse, 2004.

http://ec.europa.eu/enlargement/key_documents/cards_reports_and_publications_en.htm
—. Feasibility Report on the preparedness of Bosnia and Herzegovina to negotiate a Stabilisation and Association Agreement with the European Union, 2003, http://eurlex.europa.eu/smartapi/cgi/sga_doc?smartapi!celexplus!prod!CELEXnumdoc&lg=en&numdoc=503DC0692
—. Opinion on Croatia's Application for Membership of the EU, 2004, http://ec.europa.eu/enlargement/croatia/key_documents_en.htm
—. 2005 Enlargement Strategy and Progress Reports, available at: http://eurlex.europa.eu/smartapi/cgi/sga_doc?smartapi!celexplus!prod!CELEXnumdoc&lg=en&numdoc=505DC0561
—. 2005 Progress Report on Bosnia and Herzegovina, http://ec.europa.eu/enlargement/bosnia_and_herzegovina/key_documents_en.htm
—. 2005 Progress Report on Croatia, http://ec.europa.eu/enlargement/archives/key_documents/reports_2005_en.htm
—. 2006 Enlargement Strategy and Progress Reports, available at: http://ec.europa.eu/enlargement/key_documents/reports_nov_2006_en.htm
—. 2006 Progress Report on Bosnia and Herzegovina, http://ec.europa.eu/enlargement/bosnia_and_herzegovina/key_documents_en.htm
—. 2006 Progress Report on Croatia, http://ec.europa.eu/enlargement/key_documents/reports_nov_2006_en.htm
—. 2007 Enlargement Strategy and Progress Reports, available at: http://ec.europa.eu/enlargement/key_documents/reports_nov_2007_en.htm
—. 2007 Progress Report on Bosnia and Herzegovina, http://ec.europa.eu/enlargement/bosnia_and_herzegovina/key_documents_en.htm
—. 2007 Progress Report on Croatia, http://ec.europa.eu/enlargement/key_documents/reports_nov_2007_en.htm
—. (1993) conclusions, Copenhagen European Council, 21-22 June, para. 7 (iii). Available at: http://europa.eu/european_council/conclusions/index_en.htm

European Council conclusions on the principle of conditionality governing the development of the EU's relations with certain countries of south east Europe, 1997, http://europa.eu/bulletin/cn/9704/p202001.htm

European Council Conclusions on 'The Development of a Comprehensive Policy Based on the Commission Communication on 'The Stabilisation and Association Process for the Countries of South-Eastern Europe' Brussels 21 June 1999, http://www.consilium.europa.eu/ueDocs/cms_Data/docs/pressdata/en/gena/09008.EN9.htm

European Council conclusions, Santa Maria de Feira European Council - 19 and 20 June 2000 http://www.consilium.europa.eu/ueDocs/cms_Data/docs/pressdata/en/ec/00200-r1.en0.htm

European Council conclusions, Zagreb European Council, 24 November 2000 http://ec.europa.eu/enlargement/enlargement_process/accession_process/how_does_a_country_join_the_eu/sap/zagreb_summit_en.htm

The Thessaloniki Agenda for the Western Balkans, 16 June 2003 http://ec.europa.eu/enlargement/enlargement_process/accession_process/how_does_a_country_join_the_eu/sap/thessaloniki_agenda_en.htm

European Council conclusions, EU-Western Balkans Summit – Declaration, Thessaloniki, 21 June 2003, http://ec.europa.eu/enlargement/enlargement_process/accession_process/how_does_a_country_join_the_eu/sap/thessaloniki_summit_en. htm

Articles and books

Roberto Belloni (2007) 'Europeanization and Conflict Management in the Balkans: Lessons, Prospects, and Perils', Paper presented at the ECPR conference, Pisa, 6-8 September 2007

Tanja Borzel and Thomas Risse (2004) 'One Size Fits All! EU politics for the promotion of Human Rights, Democracy and the Rule Law, Workshop on Democracy Promotion, available at: www.atasp.de/downloads/tandt_stanford_final.pdf

Sumantra Bose (2002) *Bosnia after Dayton: nationalist partition and international intervention*, London: C. Hurst,

Marie-Janine Calic (2005) 'The Western Balkans on the Road towards European Integration, Friedrich Ebert Stiftung

Richard Caplan (2007) *Europe and the Recognition of the New States in Yugoslavia*, Cambridge: Cambridge University Press

Nicola Casarini and Costanza Musu (2007) (eds) *European foreign policy in an evolving international system : the road towards convergence*, Basingstoke: Palgrave

Spyros Economides (2001) 'In search of coherence – the Stability Pact for the Balkans' in Antonio Missiroli (ed.) *Coherence for European Security Policy: Debates, Cases Assessments*, Institute for Security Studies, Western European Union.

Michael Emerson, Senem Aydin, Julia De Clerck-Sachsse and Gergana Noutcheva, 'Just what is this 'absorption capacity' of the European Union?', CEPS Policy Brief, October 2006, available at: http://shop.ceps.eu/BookDetail.php?item_id=1381

Misha Glenny (1996) *The Fall of Yugoslavia: the third Balkan War*, London: Penguin

James Gow (1997) *Triumph of the lack of will: international diplomacy and the Yugoslav War*, New York: Columbia University Press

Heather Grabbe (2006) *The EU's transformative power: Europeanization through conditionality in Central and Eastern Europe*, Basingstoke: Palgrave

James Hughes and Gwendolyn Sasse (2003) 'Monitoring the Monitors: EU Enlargement Conditionality and Minority Protection in the CEECs,' *Journal on Ethnopolitics and Minority Issues in Europe 1*, no. 1, pp. 1-37.

James Hughes, Gwendolyn Sasse and Claire Gordon (2004) *Europeanization and Regionalization in the EU's Enlargement to Central and Eastern Europe: The Myth of Conditionality*, Basingstoke: Palgrave

Rory Keane (2004) 'The Solana Process in Serbia and Montenegro: Coherence in EU Foreign Policy', *International peacekeeping*, vol. 11, no. 3, pp. 491-507.

Noel Malcolm (1996) *Bosnia: A Short History*, Macmillan

Alan Mayhew (1998) *Recreating Europe: the European Union's policy towards central and eastern Europe*, Cambridge, Cambridge University Press

SCSP Constituent Document, 1999, http://www.stabilitypact.org/constituent/990610-cologne.asp

Stefania Panebianco and Rosa Rossi (2004) 'EU attempts to export norms of good governance to the Mediterranean and Western Balkan countries', Jean Monnet Working Papers in Comparative and International Politics

David Phinnemore and Peter Siani-Davies (2003) 'Beyond intervention? The Balkans, the Stability Pact and the European Union in Peter Siani-

Davies (ed.) *International Intervention in the Balkans since 1995*, London, Routledge, 172-193.

Christian Pippan (2004) 'The Rocky Road to Europe: The EU's Stabilisation and Association Process for the Western Balkans and the Principle of Conditionality', *European Foreign Affairs Review* 9, 219-245.

Gwendolyn Sasse (2005) 'EU Conditionality and Minority Rights: Translating the Copenhagen Criterion into Policy' EUI Working Paper No. 2005/16

—. (2004) 'Minority Rights and EU Enlargement: Normative Overstretch or Effective Conditionality', in Gabriel Toggenburg (ed), *Minority Protection and the EU: The Way Forward*, Budapest: LGI, Open Society Institute, pp. 61-84

Ulrich Schneckener (2002) 'Developing and Applying EU Crisis Management: Test Case Macedonia', ECMI Working Paper 14

Karen Smith (2003) 'The Evolution and Application of EU Membership' in Marise Cremona (ed.) *The Enlargement of the European Union*, Oxford: Oxford University Press

Nathalie Tocci (2007) *The EU and conflict resolution: promoting peace in the backyard*, London: Routledge

Gabriel Toggenburg (2006) A Remaining Share or a New Part? The Union's Role vis-à-vis Minorities After the Enlargement Decade, EUI 2006/15, http://hdl.handle.net/1814/4428

M. Uvalic (2001) 'Regional Cooperation in Southeast Europe', Journal of Southeast European and Black Sea Studies, vol. 1, no. 1, 55-75.

Milada Vachudova (2004)' Strategies for Democratisation and European Integration in the Balkans' in Marise Cremona (ed.) *The Enlargement of the European Union*, Oxford, Oxford University Press, 141-160

Marc Weller and Stefan Wolff (2005) (eds) *Autonomy, Self-governance and Conflict Resolution: Innovative approaches to institutional design in divided societies*, London: Routledge

Stefan Wolff and Anne Marie Rodt (2007) EU Reactive Crisis Management in the Western Balkans, MIRICO Report

Susan L Woodward (1995) *Balkan Tragedy: Chaos and Dissolution after the Cold War*, Washington, The Brookings Institution

Miroslav Zivanovic (2006) 'Bosnia and Herzegovina and Euro-integrations: The Case of 'Significant Progress' on Human Rights Fronts' in Imeri, Shpend (ed) *Balkan Yearbook of Human Rights 2006* http://www.balkan-rights.net/images/stories/doc/yearbook2006.pdf

CHAPTER SIX

BULGARIAN PARTICIPATION IN EMU: WHO WINS AND WHO LOSES?

LEILA SIMONA TALANI

Abstract

Bulgaria joined the EU in January 2007. In contrast to what is widely assumed, the country will not adopt the euro as its new currency immediately because it first has to show that its economy has converged with the economy of the euro-zone. Once Bulgaria has achieved economic and budgetary results which prove that its economy has converged, it will join the single currency in accordance with the procedures laid down in the Treaty.

This chapter investigates on the impact of entry on socio-economic actors and on its distributional consequences. The main research question is:

Who wins and who loses in Bulgaria from participation in EMU?

Introduction

Bulgaria joined the EU in January 2007. In contrast to what is generally assumed, the country did not adopt the euro as its new currency immediately. First its economy has to converge with the economy of the euro-zone. Once Bulgaria has achieved economic and budgetary results which prove that its economy has converged, it will join the single currency in accordance with the procedures laid down in the Treaty.

This chapter intends to investigate the impact of entry on socio-economic actors and on its distributional consequences. The main research question is:

Who wins and who loses in Bulgaria from participation in EMU?

The paper is divided into four sections. The first section reviews the institutional conditions of participation in Economic and Monetary Union (EMU)for accession countries and assesses the position of Bulgaria. The second section establishes the theoretical background. It explores different political economy approaches to European monetary integration and monetary policy-making and defines the theoretical context for assessing who wins and who loses in Bulgaria from the adoption of the euro. The third section gathers the evidence on the position of Bulgarian societal actors vis-à-vis the euro. It proposes an evaluation of Bulgarian participation in EMU on the basis of its distributional consequences. The final section concludes by proposing some explanation of the evidence proposed in the previous section in the light of the theoretical framework adopted.

1. The Institutional conditions for participation in EMU

1.1 Bulgaria and the enlargement of the euro-zone

The establishment of EMU is a major institutional undertaking whose economic consequences are not only constrained, but also defined by its institutional framework. This is to say that the economic consequences of EMU on Bulgaria are specific to the way in which this particular currency union has been devised and this, in turn, is the product of a unique historical process.

In institutional terms, the Maastricht treaty and its protocols resolved the long-lasting controversy between the 'monetarist' and the 'economist'[1] approaches to monetary union. This was made possible on the one hand through the establishment of a rigid institutional framework with a clear-cut economic objective (that of pursuing price stability) and a three-stage timetable for achieving EMU, and on the other hand by devising a set of convergence requirements which applicant Member States had to respect

[1] The distinction between "monetarists" and "economists" emerged over the course of the discussions concerning the Werner Plan and referred to the strategy to be adopted during the transitional period. The "monetarists" stressed the importance of achieving exchange rate stability through European institutional arrangements, while the "economists" pointed to the necessity of policy co-ordination and, ultimately, convergence before agreeing on the adoption of a European fixed exchange rate regime or a currency union. For more details see Tsoukalis L., (1997), The Political Economy of the European Union, Oxford University Press.

before entering. The new Member States, unlike Denmark and the United Kingdom, do not have an opt-out clause and are currently members of the Economic and Monetary Union with a "derogation" within the meaning of Article 122 EC[2]. This means that they are expected to adopt the euro once they fulfil the convergence criteria. The legal framework defining the conditions for entry of the New Member States includes the following provisions:

1. Article 122 (3) EC, which sets out the provisions of the Treaty which do not apply to the Member States with a "derogation":
2. Articles 104(9) and (11), which lay down the procedure for giving a Member State formal notice to reduce its budget deficit and makes it possible for the Council to impose financial and other penalties on Member States which persistently fail to comply;
3. certain monetary policy provisions, which remain the responsibility of Member States with a derogation;
4. certain articles concerning the European System of Central Banks (ESCB) and the European Central Bank (ECB);
5. rights and obligations under the ESCB as set out in its Statute (Article 43 ESCB)[3].

The path towards adoption of the euro is embedded in a well-defined multilateral institutional framework and includes three phases.

The first phase starts with EU membership and finishes with the country joining the Exchange Rate Mechanism II (ERM II or "new" ERM). In this phase, the Member States concerned continue to be fully responsible for their monetary and exchange rate policies. However, EU Member States are required to treat their exchange rate policies as a matter of common interest and pursue price stability as the primary objective of monetary policy. More generally, during this phase, the Member States are expected to undertake major policy adjustments, such as to implement a credible fiscal consolidation path and to advance with price liberalisation, in order to prepare already for the next steps of monetary integration.

---

[2] For the text of the article see European Union, "Consolidated version of the Treaty establishing the European Community" *Official Journal C 325 of 24 December 2002,* in the following web-site:
http://europa.eu.int/eurlex/lex/en/treaties/dat/12002E/htm/C_2002325EN.003301.html As accessed on February 7th, 2008

[3] See The European Central Bank web-site,
http://www.ecb.int/home/html/index.en.html as accessed on February 7th, 2008

The second phase involves participation in ERM II. The mechanism defines a regime characterised by fixed, but adjustable, exchange rates, with a mutually agreed central rate against the euro and a standard fluctuation band of 15%. The euro plays a central role as the anchor currency in the mechanism. As regards the entry conditions for ERM II, there are no legal criteria to be met beforehand. Thus, participation can be requested at any time by a Member State. As regards the length of participation, the Treaty foresees a minimum of two years prior to the examination of convergence. This should certainly not prevent a Member State from remaining within the mechanism for more than two years, if this is deemed to be supportive in accompanying real and nominal convergence. As far as Bulgaria and its monetary integration plans are concerned, it is important to note that ERM II can accommodate features of a number of exchange rate regimes, including currency boards, so that countries operating currency boards (like Bulgaria) might not be required to go through a double regime shift. It should be stressed, however, that participation in ERM II with a currency board is regarded as an entirely unilateral commitment by the respective country. It involves no obligations whatsoever on the part of the ECB.

The third phase is the period between the fulfilment of the Maastricht convergence criteria and the eventual adoption of the euro. In order to qualify to join the euro area, each country must achieve a high degree of sustainable economic and legal convergence. When assessing the state of economic convergence, the ECB makes use of a common framework of analysis based on the Maastricht convergence criteria. These requirements included participation in the 'new' ERM (within 15% bands) for at least two years; inflation rates no more than 1.5% higher than the average of the three most virtuous member-states; interest rates no more than 2% higher than the average of the three most virtuous member-states; a debt-to-GDP ratio not exceeding 60%, subject to conditions; and, most importantly a deficit to GDP ratio not exceeding 3% (TEU art. 104(c) and art. 109 (j))[4].

In addition, a range of backward and forward-looking indicators are used to back up the analysis, which is done in the so-called Convergence Reports. These Reports are prepared regularly by both the European Commission and the ECB.

For those countries which comply with the convergence criteria, more practical arrangements will have to be set in motion to prepare for the

[4] For the relevant articles see European Union, Treaty on European Union, Journal C 191, 29 July 1992, in http://europa.eu.int/eurlex/lex/en/treaties/dat/11992M/htm/11992M.html#0001000001 as accessed on February 7th, 2008

adoption of the euro. Once the ECOFIN Council has decided that an EU Member State outside the euro-area can adopt the euro, the country needs for example to prepare the cash changeover and the full integration of its central bank into the euro system[5].

The accession procedure involves the Council, which meets at Head of State and Government level, reaching a decision after examining the convergence reports submitted by the Commission and the ECB, having also consulted the European Parliament. It decides, on a qualified-majority basis and on a proposal from the Commission, which Member States with a derogation meet the necessary conditions for adoption of the single currency on the basis of the criteria laid down in Article 121, ending the derogation of the Member States in question.

Once this decision has been taken, the Council sets the irrevocable conversion rate between the national currency in question and the euro. This decision is taken unanimously by the Member States which have adopted the euro and the Member State in question[6].

1.2 How is Bulgaria faring on the path to the euro?

The European Commission's Comprehensive Monitoring Report for 2005 on Bulgaria[7] marks clearly the difference between the institutional realm, where shortcomings are stressed, and the economic preparation which is judged more positively. It notes, for instance, that the rule of law must be strengthened and that more should be done to combat corruption and organised crime. The economy, on the other hand, is described as having "a high degree of macroeconomic stability with strong economic growth, relatively low inflation and falling unemployment"[8]. Moreover, it

---

[5] See Trichet, J.C., (2006), Looking at EU and euro area enlargement from a central banker's angle: the views of the ECB, Speech held at Diplomatic Institute of Sofia, 27 February 2006.
http://www.ecb.int/press/key/date/2006/html/sp060227.en.html as accessed on February 2nd, 2007

[6] See ECB web-site, http://www.ecb.int/home/html/index.en.html as accessed on February 7th, 2008

[7] See European Commission, Bulgaria and Romania Monitoring Report, September 2006, in
http://ec.europa.eu/enlargement/key_documents/reports_sept_2006_en.htm
as accessed on February 8th, 2008

[8] See European Commission, Bulgaria and Romania Monitoring Report, September 2006, in
http://ec.europa.eu/enlargement/key_documents/reports_sept_2006_en.htm
as accessed on February 8th, 2008

states that continuing the current pace of reform will make the economy resilient to competitive pressure and market forces within the EU.

There are two aspects of this preparatory process that seem to be particularly important.

First, the introduction of a currency board arrangement in 1998 was a significant decision on Bulgaria's path towards economic and monetary stability and, therefore, towards EMU.

Second, with a currency board in place, monetary policy becomes entirely endogenous. Accordingly, the only macroeconomic management tools at the disposal of policy-makers are fiscal policy, labour mobility and labour market flexibility. The conduct of fiscal policyp in Bulgaria has complied with the Maastricht criteria and the Stability and Growth Pact (SGP). The deficit and debt performance between 1997 and 2005, was such that the budget position remained consistently close to balance[9].

Table 6. 1 Bulgaria: Budget deficit

Year	2000	2001	2002	2003	2004	2005
% of GDP	-0.5	0.2	-0.8	-0.1	-0.7	-1.0

Source: European Commission

Also, the government debt was well within the 60% debt to GDP rule set at Maastricht[10].

[9] See European Commission, Bulgaria and Romania Monitoring Report, September 2006, in
http://ec.europa.eu/enlargement/key_documents/reports_sept_2006_en.htm
as accessed on February 8th, 2008. For more recent data and projections see European Commission, General Government Data, Autumn 2007 in
http://ec.europa.eu/economy_finance/indicators/general_government_data/2007/ggd01_112007en.pdf as accessed on February 8th, 2008

[10] See European Commission, Bulgaria and Romania Monitoring Report, September 2006, in
http://ec.europa.eu/enlargement/key_documents/reports_sept_2006_en.htm
as accessed on February 8th, 2008. For more recent data and projections see European Commission, General Government Data, Autumn 2007 in
http://ec.europa.eu/economy_finance/indicators/general_government_data/2007/ggd01_112007en.pdf as accessed on February 8th, 2008

Table 6. 2 Bulgaria: Government debt

Year	2000	2001	2002	2003	2004	2005
% of GDP	73.6	66.2	53.2	46.2	44.4	43.2

Source: European Commission

Besides these successes, there are also challenges. Growing external imbalances are seen as a possible cause for concern. This dynamic has been largely fed by robust credit growth in the private sector. In this context, the Bulgarian National Bank (BNB) limited credit growth for banks, imposing higher reserve requirements which could impair aggregate demand and lead to recession[11].

However inflation is a major challenge on the road to future EMU membership after entry into the European Union. Indeed, at 7.6 in 2007, the harmonised index of consumer prices (HICP average annual change) is high[12].

That there remains a lot to be done in order to bring inflation fully under control is illustrated by its volatility over the recent years, falling from 10.3% in 2000 to 2.3% in 2003, followed by a subsequent increase.[13] In the next section the consequences for Bulgarian membership of the euro will be assessed.

[11] See Bulgarian National Bank, Macroeconomic indicators, in http://www.bnb.bg/bnb/home.nsf/fsWebIndex?OpenFrameset as accessed on February 8th 2008

[12] See Bulgarian National Bank, Macroeconomic indicators, in http://www.bnb.bg/bnb/home.nsf/fsWebIndex?OpenFrameset as accessed on February 8th 2008

[13] Trichet, J.C., (2006), Looking at EU and euro area enlargement from a central banker's angle: the views of the ECB, Speech held at Diplomatic Institute of Sofia, 27 February 2006. http://www.ecb.int/press/key/date/2006/html/sp060227.en.html (02/02/07)

2. The distributional consequences of EMU from a theoretical perspective

The theoretical debate over the question of the European integration is characterised by the dichotomy between the neo-functionalist approach and the intergovernmental one.[14]

The neo functionalist integration theory finds direct expression in the European Community, since it was the community itself in its early stages which was the inspiration for the thesis in the form in which it was originally offered by E.B. Haas in his study "The uniting of Europe".[15]

Neo-functionalist explanations of integration are based on the argument of spill-overs, that is that integration in one issue area will show up functional linkages to other issue areas. As a result, the desire to obtain the full benefits of integration in the first area will lead to pressures for integration in a second related area.

In fact, neo-functionalists identify two kinds of spill-over, each of which deepens and widens integration by working through interest group pressure, public opinion, elite socialisation or other domestic actors and processes. The first, functional, spill-over is economic and occurs when incomplete integration undermines the ability to achieve all the benefits of existing policies, both in the areas that are already integrated and in related sectors of economy, thus automatically creating the need for further co-operation among the EC countries. The second, political spill-over, is linked to the fundamental role of existing EC institutions in giving an impetus to a self-reinforcing process of institution building.

If applied to the issue of European Economic and Monetary Union, the spill-over proposition implies that the 1992 single-market process increased the level of support among public opinion and EC governments for all EC initiatives which could enhance the gains flowing from the single-market program.

On the other hand, the intergovernmentalist integration theory argues that nation-states dominate EC politics and that outcomes directly reflect the interests and relative power of the Member States. Bargaining at the European level is the result of strategies pursued by rational governments acting on the basis of their preferences and power. The weakest states are induced to accept undesired policies through “side-payments”.

---

[14] See Sandholtz, W., (1993), "Choosing Union: monetary politics and Maastricht" in *International Organization*, Vol. 47, pp. 1-39

[15] See Haas, E.B., (1958), *The uniting of Europe: political, social and economic forces*, Stanford, California: Stanford University Press

A meaningful example of the intergovernmentalist view is given by Andrew Moravcsik in a 1991 article, "Negotiating the Single European Act", in which he proposes an intergovernmental institutional approach to European integration[16].

As Moravcsik himself claims,[17] intergovernmental institutionalism is based on realist assumptions. States are the principal actors of the international system; inter-state bargains reflect national interests and relative power; international regimes shape inter-state politics by providing a common framework that reduces the uncertainty and transaction costs of inter-state interactions.

An attempt to explain EMU negotiations from an intergovernmental point of view has been made by David Andrews, who traces back the origins of the Maastricht agreement to a confluence of interests between the French and the German governments.[18]

The debate between neo-functionalist and intergovernmentalist theories of European integration reflects the long-standing one between neo-institutionalist and neo-realist explanations of international events and agreements.

As Hix points out,[19] both neo-functionalist and neo-realist approaches provide for agent-based accounts of international commitments, the main differences being in the identification of the agents of integration.

Indeed, where neo-functionalists trace back the origins of international and supranational commitments in the interests of national and European level interest groups[20], intergovernmentalists emphasise the

---

[16] See Moravcsik, A., (1991), "Negotiating the Single European Act: national interests and conventional statecraft in the European Community", in *International Organization,* Vol. 45, No.1, Winter 1991

[17] See Moravcsik, A., (1991), p.27

[18] See Andrews, D.M., (1993), "The global origins of the Maastricht Treaty on EMU: closing the window of opportunity", in Cafruny, A. and Rosenthal G.G., (1993), *The state of the European Community: the Maastricht debate and beyond*, Longman: Lynne Rienner Publishers. See also Andrews, D.M., (1994), "Capital mobility and state autonomy: toward a structural theory of international monetary relations", in *International Studies Quarterly*, N. 38, p.193-218

[19] See Hix, S., (1994), "The study of the European Community: the challenge to comparative politics", West European Politics 17(1): 1-30

[20] In Haas's conception interest groups are more important than parties: they are the dynamic element of political processes in advanced pluralist democracies, and this is especially true of the groups which operate in the economic sector. See Haas, E.B., (1958), p.5.

interests of the states in a state-centric, systemic study of international events[21].

However, the state-centric assumption of realist approaches has become particularly difficult to sustain also in the light of the revival of domestic approaches, or inside-out approaches to international phenomena.

More recently, many scholars come to believe that a more comprehensive and complete explanation of international events must imply the analysis of the domestic process of interest formation.

Indeed, the almost exclusive international focus of systemic approaches is problematic because it rests on a series of unexamined assumptions about domestic politics that are crucial to the result[22].

Important assumptions are made mainly in three areas: the determination of pay-off structures, or the national interests of states, the strategies available to states to alter systemic conditions, and the capacity of states to ratify and implement co-operative arrangements.

Domestic political considerations help to solve the problem of unfounded assumptions in these areas in the following three important respects.

First, a domestic politics approach allows us to determine how preferences are aggregated and national interests defined since, irrespective of whether the focus is on absolute gains or on relative gains, a theory of domestic politics offers the only way of calculating gains and losses.

Second, an analysis of the domestic situation can help explain the strategies that states adopt in order to realise their goals. It is true that strategies may be suggested by a state's structural position in the international environment, but the nature of its political system, bureaucratic politics, the influence of special interest and pressure groups and, in some issues, even public opinion may ultimately determine which strategies states can pursue internationally.

Third, internationally agreed terms must always be enforced internally in order to become effective. Thus, since domestic ratification is essential, when negotiating internationally, policy makers must always anticipate domestic reactions: international agreements can always be reached, but they can only be implemented if the domestic actors concur.

---

[21] See Moravcsik, A., (1991).

[22] See Milner, H., (1992), "Theories of cooperation", in *World Politics*, Vol. 44, pp. 427-495. See also Milner, H., (1993), "The assumption of anarchy in IR theory: a critique" in Baldwin, D.A., (1993), *Neo-realism and neo-liberalism: the contemporary debate*, Columbia University Press

For these reasons, domestic politics are essential in order to understand international co-operation and international economic co-operation in particular.[23]

Moving out of US academic circles toward the European debate on the issue of European integration it is necessary to give an account of the attempt made by Simon Bulmer to transfer Katzenstein's integrated international-domestic politics approach from foreign economic policy issues to the problems of European policy.[24]

This need has also been addressed by Moravcsik himself who has built on his preceding institutional intergovernmentalist approach to create a new "liberal intergovernmentalism". The latter approach refines the theory of inter-state bargaining and institutional compliance and adds an explicit theory of national preference formation grounded in liberal theories of international interdependence.[25]

At the core of liberal intergovernmentalism are three essential elements: the assumption of rational state behaviour, a liberal theory of national preference formation, and an intergovernmentalist analysis of inter-state negotiation.

The model of rational state behaviour on the basis of domestically constrained preferences implies that international conflict and co-operation can be modelled as a process that takes place in two successive stages. First, governments define a set of interests, and then bargain among themselves in an effort to realise those interests.

This shift toward a two-level approach to the study of international relations is completed by Moravcsik in his introduction to Evans, Jacobson and Putnam's book "Double edged diplomacy: international bargaining and domestic politics".[26]

---

[23] See Milner, H., (1992), "Theories of cooperation", in *World Politics*, Vol. 44, pp. 427-495. See also Milner, H., (1993), "The assumption of anarchy in IR theory: a critique" in Baldwin, D.A., (1993), *Neo-realism and neo-liberalism: the contemporary debate*, Columbia University Press

[24] See Bulmer , S., (1983), "Domestic politics and European Community policy-making", in Journal of Common Market Studies, Vol. XXI, No. 4, June 1983, p. 354. For further references, see Rosamond, B., "Mapping the European condition: the theory of integration and the integration of theory", European Journal of International Relations, 1995, Vol. 1 (3): 391-408

[25] See Moravcsik, A., (1993)a, "Preferences and power in the EC: a liberal intergovernmentalist approach", *Journal of Common Market Studies*, vol. 31, No. 4, December 1993, p. 474

[26] See Moravcsik, A., (1993)b, "Integrating international and domestic theories of international bargaining" in Evans, P.B., Jacobson, H.K., Putnam, R.D., (1993),

Here the author acknowledges that the question facing international relation theorists today is no longer whether to combine domestic and international explanations into a theory of double-edged diplomacy, but how best to do it, and the answer to this question is found in Putnam's two-level games theory.[27]

Indeed, in his article "Diplomacy and Domestic Politics",[28] Putnam provided of the most well-known attempts to find an integrated domestic-international politics approach to international agreements.

Putnam's approach to the problem rests on the metaphor of the two-level game for domestic-international relations. At the national level, domestic groups pursue their interests by pressuring governments to adopt favourable policies, and politicians seek power by constructing coalitions among these groups. At the international level, national governments seek to maximise their own ability to satisfy domestic pressures, while minimising the adverse consequences of foreign developments. Since each national political leader appears at both game boards, international relations scholars cannot ignore either of the two games.

However, it is Jeffrey Frieden, in his "Invested interests: the politics of national economic policies in a world of global finance"[29] who provides for the application of Putnam's two-level game to the issue of international exchange rate commitments. In particular, he identifies the main domestic interests at stake in the two interrelated issues of exchange rate level and regimes, thus proposing the bases for a socio-economic definition of the sources of exchange rate commitments credibility.

According to Frieden, two interrelated dimensions of policy choice are especially important in an environment of increasing capital mobility as the European Community has been over the last twenty years[30]: the degree of exchange rate flexibility and the level of the exchange rate itself.

Double-edged diplomacy: international bargaining and domestic policy, Berkeley: University of California Press

[27] See Moravcsik, A., (1993)b, p. 9

[28] See Putnam, R., (1988), "Diplomacy and domestic politics", in International Organization, Vol. 42.

[29] See Frieden, J., (1991), "Invested interests: the politics of national economic policies in a world of global finance", in *International Organization*, N. 45, Autumn 1991; see also Frieden, J., (1994), *The impact of goods and capital market integration on European monetary politics*, Preliminary version, August 1994

[30] Incidentally, the issue of European monetary Union was addressed for the first time in the context of the European community precisely at the beginning of the '70s, with the Werner plan, since the Treaty of Rome, in its original version, did not contain any reference to the goal of monetary union. Although many authors, such as Padoa Schioppa (see Padoa-Schioppa, T., (1988), "The European monetary

With regard to the first dimension, in a Mundell-Fleming world[31] with full capital mobility, a country faces something of a trade-off between exchange rate stability and monetary policy autonomy[32].

Thus, while some actors may favour a low degree of exchange rate flexibility, others will be willing to accept a higher degree of exchange rate flexibility, ranging from a freely floating rate solution to a two-tier EMU.

Regarding the second dimension - the preferred level of exchange rates - some fixing of the exchange rate is assumed, as was the case in the EMS before the crisis. However, some actors will prefer a high, more appreciated, exchange rate, while others will prefer a low, more depreciated, one.

The constellation of interests involved in the negotiation and implementation phases of exchange rate commitments according to Frieden's model can be simplified as follows:

system: a long term view", in Giavazzi, F., Micossi, S. and Miller, M., (1988), The European Monetary System, Cambridge: Cambridge University Press), claim that this was due to the collapse of the Bretton Wood system, some evidence may be found that this debate over monetary arrangements was urged by the growing impact of greater capital mobility. See, for references on this subject, Bank for International Settlement (BIS), (1990), *Sixtieth Annual report*, Basle: BIS

[31] The Mundell-Fleming model is a macroeconomic model which brings together the monetary equilibrium, that is, the equilibrium of the monetary set of variables (given by the equilibrium between the money supply and demand) illustrated in the so-called LM curve, and the real variables equilibrium (the equilibrium between investments and savings) in the so-called IS curve. The model also includes the equilibrium of the external economic relationships in the form of the balance of payments equilibrium, as shown in the so-called BP curve. For further explanation of the model see Gandolfo, G., (1989), *Corso di economia internazionale*, UTET LIBRERIA, ch.18

[32] See also Padoa-Schioppa, T., (1988)

Table 6. 3 Frieden's Model

	FLOATING EXCHANGE RATES	FIXED EXCHANGE RATES	
DEPRECIATION OF THE CURRENCY	Manufacturing, small companies	Export-oriented, big companies	Manufacturing, small companies + Export oriented, big companies
APPRECIATION OF THE CURRENCY	Public sector	Financial and banking sector	Public sector + financial and banking sector
	Manufacturing, small companies, + Public sector	Export-oriented, big companies + financial and banking sector	

The application of this model to Bulgaria will help to define who wins and who loses from the process of Economic and monetary Union. In macroeconomic terms, the coalition of multinational companies and the big financial and banking sectors should obtain the highest benefits from joining EMU. By contrast, small manufacturing companies would lose their competitive edge, especially if the country experiences a high degree of inflation before entry.

3. The distributional effects and macroeconomic impact of Bulgaria joining the euro: Hypotheses and evidence

3.1 Evaluating the impact of joining EMU on different socio-economic sectors

The path to participation in a monetary union has important implications for domestic economic policies which in turn often require the implementation of comprehensive structural reforms. These in particular involve constraints on the use of national fiscal policy as an anti-cyclical tool and the consequent stress on the flexibility of labour markets and labour mobility[33]. Similarly, product and capital markets are likely to undergo profound changes.

Starting with fiscal policy, expenditure and revenue structure may be redesigned in a way that reduces public spending and the burden of the welfare state first by respecting the Maastricht criteria, and second through adherence to the Stability and Growth Pact (SGP) . This is likely to produce winners and losers, the latter in particular consisting of less privileged social strata and groups.

Regarding labour markets, a major challenge for structural reforms is to find the right balance between social considerations and individual incentives which maximise economic welfare. Areas of particular interest are social transfer systems, employment protection laws and wage-setting mechanisms, including wage indexation, which all risk being substantially transformed if not abolished. Equally likely to be implemented are policies supporting the creation of new businesses. From the monetary policy point of view it would also be possible for labour market reforms to be shaped in such a way as to allow for wage adjustments that reflect more closely regional and sectoral productivity differences.[34]

Turning to product market reforms, the opening up of the markets will leave the way open for foreign capital to enter and substantially modify the Bulgarian productive structure as the adoption of the single market will eliminate existing barriers to free competition. This will have an impact on domestic small and medium-sized firms and business, marginalising those which are very likely to succumb to competitive pressures.

As far as financial markets are concerned, structural reforms are advocated which aim to facilitate a more effective allocation of savings toward the most rewarding investment opportunities, and at the same time to secure financial stability. Greater financial integration and the modernisation of the financial system will facilitate the entry of international financial actors into Bulgarian capital markets and the provision of financial and other services by foreign capital.

---

[33] See Talani, L.S., 2004, European Political Economy, Political Science Perspectives, London: Ashgate.

[34] Stark, J.,(2006)," Economic and monetary challenges of euro area enlargement", Dinner speech held at the conference "The changing landscape of FDI in Europe" organised by the Oesterreichische Nationalbank Vienna, 20 November 2006 http://www.ecb.int/press/key/date/2006/html/sp061120.en.html

In conclusion therefore, and adding further dimensions to Frieden's model on the socio-economic impact of entry into a currency Union, we could propose the following schema:

Table 6. 4 Winners and Losers from Bulgarian participation in EMU

	DOMESTIC	FOREIGN
WINNERS	Large-scale manufacturing sector Financial Sector	Multinational companies International financial sector
LOSERS	Small and Medium companies Trade Unions and Organised Labour	

On the basis of these considerations, it is possible to hypothesise that that the national as well as international large manufacturers and international companies will be in favour of immediate participation in EMU, whereas the small and medium domestic interests and the trade unions will be opposed. In the next section we shall discover what the actual positions of societal actors in the debate over Bulgarian entry into EMU are, with a view to verifying whether the consensus on and opposition to accession is polarised alongside the divide between winners and losers identified through the theoretical framework used.

3.2 Bulgarian societal actors: positioning themselves towards EMU participation

3.2.1 Public Debate[35]

As one might expect from the hypotheses specified above, the issue of entry into the euro is highly controversial within the Bulgarian public debate. There are high expectations alongside great pessimism about potential negative effects, e.g. expectations of impoverishment, lower disposable household income, increases in retail prices, high competitive

[35] This section is mainly based on the research notes by my research assistant Dr Plamen Rachelv whom I thank for collecting and translating all the bibliography in Bulgarian.

pressures. Overall, the Bulgarian general public, workers, and consumers feel they will be the losers in Bulgarian accession to the EMU.

Many ordinary citizens believe that after adopting the euro, prices of consumer goods will raise. In this regard, the German experience is often referred to, especially the notorious German nickname for the euro - "teuro" (which means 'expensive'). Regardless of some pessimist expectations of price increases, most Bulgarians are already used to the euro: they calculate prices in euro, buy real estate in euro, and keep savings in euro.[36]

Kaloyan Simeonov in his article entitled "Public Opinion in Bulgaria on the Road towards the euro-zone" summarises the position of general public opinion.

The article highlights three basic issues regarding the preparation for adoption of the euro. The first issue focuses on the type of exchange-rate regime which Bulgaria will apply until accession to the euro-zone. The following scenarios are included in the study: a static scenario with a retention of the currency board, two scenarios with participation in the exchange-rate mechanism II within a band, as well as two more extreme scenarios: managed floating with a central rate to the euro and unilateral euroisation. The second issue refers to the position of the public opinion with regards to the benefits for Bulgaria of entering the euro-zone. The third issue analyses opinions on the time framework for Bulgaria's adoption of the single currency.

Out of the five exchange rate scenarios during preparations for Bulgarian membership of the euro-zone, experts mainly support the maintenance of the currency board regime. This also coincides with the official position expressed by Bulgarian institutions.

The official opinion of the governmental institutions is that acceptance of the euro will be most beneficial from the macroeconomic point of view. However it will also represent a positive move for companies as well for Bulgarian citizens. Most experts believe that Bulgaria will be ready for membership of the euro-zone in 2009 or 2010, although there are few who say that 2011 or 2012 is also possible.

Most of the representatives of businesses, scientific circles, and other social groups prefer the policy of holding on to the currency board regime until Bulgaria's adherence to the euro-zone, and their support for other scenarios is clearly lower. However, support among the wider public for

---

36 See Европейски акценти, РФИ, 22.03.2007, http://www.rfi.bg/prog/euaccent/show.shtml?type=show&program=euaccent&news_NUM=915&indexa=no

the currency board regime is lower than the support of experts working in Bulgarian institutions.

The public at large is much more prone to unilateral 'euroisation' than experts are.

Both groups mostly believe that accepting the euro will be useful first of all on the macroeconomic level, while benefits for companies and individual citizens will be minor. It is likely that the low percentage which considers that joining the euro-zone will be useful for citizens could be related to the widely held perception that introducing the euro will result in much higher prices throughout the country. Contrary to the experts' view, there is a strong scepticism among the general public about the benefits of the introduction of the euro.

Moving now to the length of time it will take for Bulgaria to be ready to introduce the common European currency, the view again prevails that this will not occur before 2009 or 2010; however, unlike experts in the institutions, the sceptical approach that the country will be ready to join the EMU only after 2012 is much more common among general public.

Public attitudes to the introduction of the euro reveal the mixed, if not negative, feelings among the public about the future introduction of the common European currency in Bulgaria.

There are many similarities between the attitudes of experts and other social groups, i.e. that keeping the currency board not only until membership of the EU, but also until membership of the European Monetary Union, is the optimal solution for introducing the euro, or that membership of the euro-zone will be beneficial first of all at the macroeconomic level and its benefits for companies and individual citizens will not be so high. There is also a similarity in the prevailing opinions that Bulgaria will most probably be ready to introduce the euro as legal tender in 2009-2010.

There are also some important differences between attitudes of experts in Bulgarian institutions and those of other social groups, reflected in higher support throughout society for more extreme versions of exchange rate policy – the application of a regime of regulated floating exchange rates with a central exchange rate to the euro, or unilateral 'euroisation'. Among wider social groups, the percentage of those who believe that accession to the euro-zone will also be beneficial for the general public is lower, and at the same time the sceptical view that Bulgaria will be ready to introduce the euro only after 2012 is held by a higher number of citizens. This is mostly due to fears about probable price increases in Bulgaria resulting from adoption of the euro.

In conclusion, public opinion, even if it is generally unified around some key issues concerning preparation for membership of the euro-zone, is not totally consolidated on all aspects of the accession process and on future membership in the European Monetary Union. This is an argument for stimulating a more intensive public discussion on the future adoption of the common European currency, on the benefits and threats of the introduction of the euro in Bulgaria, and also on the most important challenges associated with the membership of the European Monetary Union.[37]

3.2.2 The Trade Unions

There is not yet a broad debate in Bulgaria on the impact of entry into EMU on the trade unions. The trade unions may refer to something that will happen in the future, but no workshops or official studies have yet been produced. In general, the unions are not happy about the euro, but have still to adopt a formal official position.

In an interview with Katia Iordanova (Director of the Union of transport workers- Sauz na trasortnite rabotnizi) on 22 May 2007 in Sofia, the main areas of concern of the trade unions in relation to entry into EMU emerged[38]. The Union of Transport workers is part of the European Transport Workers' Federation (ETF)[39]. Through the Bulgarian Confederation of Labour, the union represented by Mrs Iordanova is part of the European Trade Union Confederation (ETUC)[40].

The first area of concern is the impact of entry on prices and, indirectly, on Union membership.

The feeling is that 1 euro will be 1.95 lev, a first, immediate consequence of which will be that wages will lose purchasing power, simply through the effective doubling of prices.

---

[37] Simeonov, K., Public Opinion in Bulgaria on the Road towards the Eurozone, *Alternativi* Journal, UNWE, http://alternativi.unwe.acad.bg/br14/05_-_Kaloyan_Simeonov.doc

[38] Interview with Katia Iordanova (Director of the Union of transport workers- Sauz na trasortnite rabotnizi) on 22 May 2007, Sofia-Bulgaria

[39] For more information about the European Transport workers' federation see http://www.itfglobal.org/etf/ as accessed on February 8th, 2008

[40] The ETUC includes two Bulgarian national Trade Unions organisations: The *CITUB* Confederation of Independent Trade Unions of Bulgaria (see http://www.knsb-bg.org/eng/enindex.htm) and the PODKREPA Confederation of Labour (see http://www.education-cee.org/oldsite/centres/podkrepa/index.htm) to which the Federation of transport workers belong. See also ETUC web-site http://www.etuc.org/a/82 as accessed on February 8th 2008.

The euro brings lower wages and higher prices. Trade Unions are convinced that prices will double, as occurred in Germany.

Higher prices bring unemployment which means lower Union membership.

The second area of concern is the restructuring of the labour markets as related to the implementation of the Lisbon process[41]. The perception amongst the unionists is that the restructuring process in Bulgaria is moving very fast. There were many privatisations in the years before the country's entry into the EU and the impact on the trade unions and workers was particularly negative. In particular, the new processes of liberalisation and privatisation, coupled with the different forms of ownership meant that TU membership fell as was no longer compulsory.

The Unions are therefore staunchly opposed to the flexibility that the process of joining EMU will entail.

To conclude, in the opinion of Mrs Iordanova there is no doubt that multinational companies (MNCs) will win and workers will lose from entry into EMU. MNCs will win because they will have the choice to use workers who are not well paid.

However, this negative position is not shared by the representatives of private sector workers, especially those involved in tourism.

Assen Chaushev (Director of the Intermenu Academy-International Academy for VIP-Restaurant employees) advances precisely the opposite arguments of Mrs Iordanova in support of the view that entry into EMU will result in a major benefit for employees.

Although, in his view, the question of Bulgarian participation in EMU has not yet been discussed in Bulgaria, the introduction of the euro in Germany has been closely monitored. Although there have been discussions in Germany on inflation, he does not find that prices have increased. Such effects may have been apparent only at the outset. The same will happen in Bulgaria. No preparatory work is needed. Even if the euro were introduced tomorrow they would welcome it. The workers of the tourism industry will make profits because the production and redistribution of goods occurs within a competitive framework and prices will go down by themselves. The sooner the euro is introduced, the better. Such a move will not do harm or produce problems. It will help the labour markets in Bulgaria to draw closer to the European markets and especially to Bulgarians abroad in the euro area. The Central Bank of Bulgaria cannot monitor remittances but they are significant. This is why the euro is

---

[41] For the relations between the Lisbon process and EMU see Talani, L.S. et al. (ed)(2008) Back to Maastricht, CSP

a good thing. A million people living abroad support a million people living at home.[42]

As far as the impact on the internal labour market is concerned, Mr Chaushev believes that it can only be good because, due to competitive pressures, employers will increase the salaries of workers: instead of a salary of, say, 150 lev they will receive 150 euros.

As regards the flexibility of labour markets, he does not have such fears because Bulgaria has still not reached levels of flexibility such as those in Italy, although more structural reforms are discussed. In Bulgaria there are three trade unions. The biggest two are in the state sector.[43] The one he is working for, on the other hand, is focused on the private sector which is difficult to penetrate because trade unions have received a bad press in Bulgaria. This issue of flexibility has been raised, although employers are essentially at the mercy of workers, even in the absence of trade unions, because there are not enough workers, especially in the tourism sector. Therefore employers are under pressure to increase salaries and to guarantee protection. There is therefore a shortage of employees in many private sectors, including tourism, the construction sector, light industry, food processing, and textiles. Although they could not have foreseen this problem five years ago, unemployment is decreasing. Whilst there is unemployment, it is concentrated amongst people over 50 for whom it is difficult to find jobs.

Therefore it will not be MNCs which benefit from Bulgarian accession to EMU. According to Mr Chaushev, multinational companies' interest in Bulgaria has already vanished. It was high when wages where low and there were workers, but now many MNCs are going away because it is becoming too expensive. In his opinion, it is a fact that cheap labour is no longer an advantage in Bulgaria, which makes it less appealing for MNCs.

Therefore, the workers will benefit more, including both those in Bulgaria and those abroad. The introduction of the euro is not a problem, because everything is already calculated in euros anyway. Real estates is sold in euros, people think in euros, nearly half of the contracts are in euros on account of the stability of the euro[44].

---

[42] See interview to Assen Chaushev (Director of the Intermenu Academy-International Academy for VIP-Restaurant employees), held in Sofia, Bulgaria on May 22nd, 2007

[43] See note above.

[44] See interview with Assen Chaushev (Director of the Intermenu Academy-International Academy for VIP-Restaurant employees), held in Sofia, Bulgaria on May 22nd, 2007

3.2.3 The banking and financial sector

Financial and banking operators in Bulgaria are among the leading proponents of a fast adoption of the euro as a means of payment. Most refer to the currency board in Bulgaria as an indispensable step towards the ERM and the euro-zone. Rumen Avramov, an independent economic analyst, in an article published in Capital Weekly, No. 26/ 29.06.2007, advocates a speedier introduction of the euro. He argues that the initial deadline of adopting the euro by 2009-2010 has to be kept and not prolonged to 2011-2012 or 2012-2015, if the strategic advantages of the currency board are to be fully exploited. He also points out that when the government is hesitant and meek, the chances of adopting the euro in Bulgaria decrease substantially. Avramov also emphasises the need to maintain the currency board until the precise moment of Bulgaria's accession to the euro-zone. Meanwhile, he expresses concerns about what he calls “a delay in entering the ERM II”. According to him, it is disturbing that more than half a year after Bulgaria's entry into the EU the country is still far from joining the ERM II. He interprets this as a probable indication of the unwillingness of the European Central Bank to speed up the process of Bulgaria's membership of the euro-zone. Mr Avramov regards the euro-zone as a protective realm of stability for the Bulgarian economy.[45]

In the report “EMU on the Horizon” BNB Deputy Governors Tsvetan Manchev and Mincho Karavastev also advocate a fast adoption of the euro.[46]

In an interview with the author, Lyubomir Gueorgiev[47] (Chief Internal Audit Commercial Bank Tokuda) confirmed that the private banking sector is not worried about Bulgarian entry into the EMU.

As far as the preparations for the introduction of the euro are concerned, no special preparations will be needed, because the pegging of the lev to the euro within the currency board has introduced the legal framework, which therefore is already in place. As regards wholesale banking, any financial transaction at the national level within the country

---

[45] Аврамов, Р., Когато властта е мекушава, шансовете за приемане на Еврото намаляват, в. Капитал, бр. 26, 29 юни 2007, http://www.capital.bg/show.php?storyid=354200

[46] Йорданов, Б., "Банк Аустрия кредитанщалт": България може да приеме еврото около 2010 г., в. Дневник, 18.08.2005, http://evropa.dnevnik.bg/show/print.php?storyid=198755

[47] See interview to Lyubomir Gueorgiev (Chief Internal Audit Commercial Bank Tokuda) held in Sofia, Bulgaria on May 22nd, 2007

is subject to the same regime, whether it is denominated in levs or in euros. Obviously in retail banking things are still different, but it would not appear to be too problematic to shift to the new euro regime. The systems introduced regulating RTP (real time payments) for both the euro and the lev are practically identical, from the technical point of view, in terms of the financial transfers themselves, as well as from the financial point of view (apart from the standard deviation of the currency of 0.5% each way).

The deposit base of the population is regulated by the interest rates of commercial banks. These rates are the same for both deposits in euros and in lev (as well as in dollars).

One of the main concerns over the introduction of the euro is its inflationary impact.

Indeed, also according to Mr Lyubomir Gueorgiev its adoption will fuel inflation as has been the case in all other countries. Even in countries like Montenegro (which adopted the euro unilaterally) people say that prices have increased. There is a general view in Bulgaria that 1 lev will be converted into 1 euro. This will influence the market. This is a general tendency. However, the Bank of Bulgaria will not intervene because the currency board does not allow such action. Indeed, the experts from the central bank claim that because of the currency board Bulgaria is more prepared than any other country to enter the euro.

As regards the impact on the banking sector, it depends on the current market situation. Even if the euro is an element, it is not the only one. The banking sector is already almost completely owned by foreigners. Over 75% of the banking sector is already owned by EU banking groups. UNICREDIT owns 35% of the Bulgarian banking sector. A Greek group also controls a large share. The third banking group in Bulgaria is the OTP group[48] (now owned by Hungarians). Among the big banks only one is Bulgarian (First Investment Bank) although also in this case a share is owned by European investors,[49.] All the other big banks are foreign banks. In practice, the banking sector in Bulgaria is foreign. This is another argument in support of the view that the introduction of the euro will not lead to any big change in the Bulgarian banking sector. Retail banking is

---

[48] OTP Bank is the biggest bank in Hungary and a member of OTP Bank Group, one of the leading financial groups in central and eastern Europe. See OTP Bank group web-site https://www.otpbank.hu/OTP_Portal/online/CE01000000000000.jsp accessed on February 25th, 2008

[49] See First Investment Bank web-site http://www.fibank.bg accessed on February 25th 2008/

already largely carried out in euros. This means that the practical disappearance of the lev will not result in any changes. This already became clear when most deposits in deutschmarks were transformed into euros. The banking sector is already ready, and therefore no special preparations will be made.[50].

As far as the relations between the banking and the industrial sector are concerned, Bulgarian companies, mostly the medium and large enterprises, have a very lively interaction with the banking sector. Their major source of finance is still the banking sector. The stock exchange is not very well developed. Debt issue as a means of financing the industrial sector is still uncommon. In recent years there have been efforts to improve the situation, but still, only a few companies are listed. Moreover, the peculiarity of the privatisation process in Bulgaria resulted in the mass privatisation of many companies with a lot of small shareholders, which are however now consolidating and withdrawing from the stock market. The result of this was to consolidate and concentrate capital in a very small number of owners. The introduction of the euro will facilitate the access of Bulgarian capital owners to the European stock market. Because the industrial sector is still financed by the banking sector, they will switch immediately to the European market. The Bulgarian stock market will also be stimulated by Europeans buying up Bulgarian stock as well as by Bulgarian capital financing through the European stock market. Thus the introduction of the euro will stimulate the development of the Bulgarian stock market through the process of access to the European stock market. This is the view of many people in the banking sector. Will many Bulgarian companies be bought by foreign capital? Yes. The process is already underway and will be intensified as Bulgarian capital is too fragile and without the assistance of foreign capital will not be able to withstand.[51]

In conclusion, for Mr Lyubomir Gueorgiev there are certainly going to be losers, insofar as the introduction of the euro will open the door for speculation with the result that, since there is a free market, many people will speculate. There are also some less clear elements since in Bulgaria the level of salaries is a problem - i.e. they are too low. The opening up of the market could affect the salaries even further. This is also apparent in the huge section of the submerged economy where salaries are unprotected. In Bulgaria this sector is very large. The winners will be all

---

[50] See interview to Lyubomir Gueorgiev (Chief Internal Audit Commercial Bank Tokuda) held in Sofia, Bulgaria on May 22nd, 2007

[51] See interview to Lyubomir Gueorgiev (Chief Internal Audit Commercial Bank Tokuda) held in Sofia, Bulgaria on May 22nd, 2007

those who identify the euro as the symbol of free movement of capital, starting from people who will be able to exchange money to travel, through to those who will identify with a bigger European financial community.

Mr Stoyan Manolov (Director, Off-site Supervision and Analyses – Bulgarian National Bank) is even more optimistic than his colleague.[52.]

Also according to him, no specific preparations are required for the banking sector. Bulgaria has already introduced international banking regulations as of 2003. It already complies with all regulations. There are however some technicalities to be dealt with. For example, Bulgaria will become a member of the EU payment system.

Moreover, capital inflows will increase. However, Bulgaria is already fully open to the extent that already 95% of the banks assets are denominated in euros. Foreign assets and liabilities are denominated in euros. There will not be any transaction or transformation costs because the regime is fixed.

The only impact could be a currency risk, which could be reflected by the entry exchange rate, although there is already a pegged level which should be respected.

In his opinion, Bulgaria will join the ERMII in 2008 and enter EMU in 2010.

The Bulgarian banking system will not be affected by entry at all because the system is totally dominated by European Banks and assets. There is some scope for consolidation of the banking system. However local banks have their niche, and therefore this too is limited.

As far as the impact on the stock exchange is concerned, the stock exchange is not very developed; therefore there is the possibility of consolidation with other European stock exchanges. However, it is very likely that corporate financing will remain dominated by the banking sector. This will remain unchanged.[53]

In conclusion, according to Mr Stoyan Manolov no one loses from financial stability. Inflationary pressures will be offset by productivity and GDP increases and there is no way to change the exchange rate because it is determined by law.

---

[52] See interview to Stoyan Manolov (Director, Off-site Supervision and Analyses – Bulgarian National Bank), Bulgaria on May 23rd, 2007

[53] See interview to Stoyan Manolov (Director, Off-site Supervision and Analyses – Bulgarian National Bank), Bulgaria on May 23rd, 2007

3.2.4 Domestic industry

In Bulgaria national industry consists predominantly of small and medium enterprises (SMEs). They account for around 99 percent of total businesses in the country (those with at least 250 employees).[54] Besides, they are the basic national employment source with a share of total employment of 50.7 percent[55]. This was a consequence of the structural and privatisation processes which resulted in labour force reorientation from the public to the private sector. In 2001, private sector employment accounted for 60.3 percent of total employment, with the share increasing to 62.6 percent only a year later. The share of the employed in the public sector dropped down from 39.5 percent in 2001 to 37.2 percent in 2002.

The position of domestic industry in favour of a swift accession to the euro-area was discussed in an interview with Mr Oleg Yordanov (General manager of Autotrade)[56].

In his opinion, for the industrial sector favouring the euro is not so much a question of emotion as one of the level of preparation. What they learned from other European countries like Italy, Greece, and Portugal is that even these countries had difficulties, and some of the new countries delayed their entry.

It is clear from the dynamics of his sector of production that price increases will be a problem. In the last fifteen years prices have tripled due to increases in the cost of labour and materials.

The introduction of the euro will reduce the competitiveness of the Bulgarian industrial system. This is bound to happen, but should take place in a step-by-step manner in order to prevent it by increasing productivity and increasing innovation.

Although politicians and central bankers want to introduce the euro at once, this will have serious consequences for domestic industry. Indeed, although the currency board has stabilised the financial sector, it did not improve the situation of the domestic manufacturing sector which is already invaded by foreign companies, including in particular Italian companies, which exploit economic opportunities and especially low

---

[54] See Center for Economic Development, (2003), EU Enlargement and its Impact on the Social Policy and Labour Markets of Accession and Non-Accession Countries Bulgaria Country report, Sofia 2003, p. 7-9

[55] See Center for Economic Development, (2003), EU Enlargement and its Impact on the Social Policy and Labour Markets of Accession and Non-Accession Countries Bulgaria Country report, Sofia 2003, p. 7-9

[56] See interview to Oleg Yordanov (General manager of Autotrade), Bulgaria on May 23rd, 2007

wages. This is why entry should be subordinated to certain conditions and the maintenance of particular income levels (they should increase significantly) before adopting the euro.

Indeed, according to Mr Yordanov the euro is not at all a factor influencing foreign investment. Investors calculate their interest and if the income is good they will come, but they draw comparisons with the rest of the world. This does not depend on the euro. There are already plenty of foreign companies in Bulgaria, even though it has not yet adopted the single currency. Therefore more foreign investment is not expected. The euro is not the essence of economic change. Without competitive production there is not possibility for survival. The major question is whether the euro is good. This cannot be answered at the moment. Preparations are necessary. The statistics from Greece say that cost of living has increased by 40%. If this happens in Bulgaria and the euro is adopted tomorrow almost 80% of the population will have problems making ends meet.

The consequence will be that rich people win and poor people lose. The country's debt has been changed from dollars into euros. There is not therefore going to be a big change for the banks, but since their margins will increase it will be good for them. The banks will be the real winners[57].

The business community contains other vociferous opponents of early entry. Ivo Prokopiev, Chairman of the Confederation of Employers and Industrial Entrepreneurs in Bulgaria, when addressing a conference on the occasion of the Tenth Anniversary of the Currency Board in Bulgaria and Challenges before adopting the euro, said that it would be realistic to expect the adoption of the euro in Bulgaria within the next five years. He further noted that the main problem would be how to overcome the difficulties resulting from the domestic and external shocks already afflicting the Bulgarian economy. Prokopiev suggested that measures aimed at lowering income tax and social security tax payments are necessary and favorable not only for businesses but for providing general flexibility within the Bulgarian economy. He also stressed that Bulgaria needs to develop multiple economic sectors and not to rely on a single-commodity economy, which may have devastating effects if a major international crisis occurs. Prokopiev argued that at present Bulgaria would be vulnerable to such a crisis, which would hit most hardly the pivotal real estate sector and the related construction, tourism and financial services sectors. Therefore, before adopting the euro, Prokopiev advocates

---

57 See interview to Oleg Yordanov (General manager of Autotrade), Bulgaria on May 23rd, 2007

fundamental reforms to systems like education, health care, social security and the civil service.[58]

Why does the Bulgarian manufacturing sector not favour EMU?

As Frieden's model predicts, the main reasons are related to the level of the exchange rates and the elimination of the possibility of devaluing which entry into EMU would entail. Indeed, as the experience of the currency board already foreshadows, the adoption of the euro will result in an appreciation of the Bulgarian exchange rate which, given the level of Bulgarian inflation will reduce, given the inability to devalue, the competitiveness of the national industry. In the event, this could lead to the dismantlement of the national manufacturing sector and its replacement by more competitive multinational corporations. Indeed, despite the prevailing consensus in the literature that real appreciation has not, at least until recently, affected Bulgaria's competitiveness, international comparisons rank Bulgaria very low in terms of cost competitiveness among comparator accession countries.[59] Even before the nominal appreciation of the lev against the US dollar, the higher inflation in Bulgaria resulted in appreciation in real terms against the anchor currency, the euro, thus eroding Bulgaria's cost competitiveness in the euro-zone.

---

[58] Въвеждането на Еврото е реалистично да стане в рамките на следващите пет години, БНР, 18.09.2007, http://www.bnr.bg/radiobulgaria/emission_bulgarian/news/1809-6.htm

[59] Pashev, K., (2003), Competitiveness of the Bulgarian Economy, Bulgarian National Bank, Discussion Papers August 2003

Figure 6. 1 Real appreciation of the LEV

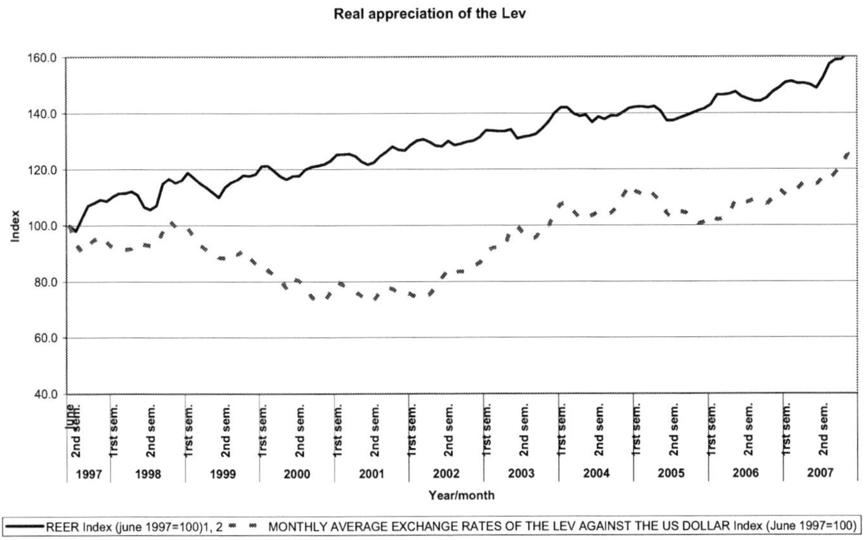

Source: Elaboration of the author on BNB data

During the years of the currency board, wages registered impressive growth in real terms, although Bulgaria's average wage remains the lowest among accession countries. Low wages certainly remain the country's most important comparative advantage, but sustaining this advantage is not easy in the global economy. Therefore, low labour costs should be replaced by productivity gains in order to increase the competitiveness of the national industry.

Figure 6. 2 Manufacturing annual average wage growth in Bulgaria, 1997-2002 (Eur, 1997=100)

	1997	**1998**	**1999**	**2000**	**2001**	**2002**
Manufacturing Total	911	1194	1243	1343	1392	1496
Nominal	100	131.1	136.5	147.4	152.8	164.2
CPI-Adjusted	100	110.4	112.1	109.8	106.0	107.7
PPI-Adjusted	100	112.8	113.8	104.6	104.5	111.0
Private sector	745	1004	1082	1280	1329	1447
Nominal	100	134.7	145.2	171.8	178.4	194.1
CPI-Adjusted	100	113.5	119.3	127.9	123.7	127.3
PPI-Adjusted	100	115.9	121.1	121.9	122.0	131.2

Source: Pashev, K., (2003), Competitiveness of the Bulgarian Economy, Bulgarian National Bank, Discussion Papers August 2003, p.36

Data from the Bulgarian National Bank show that productivity improved on average by 7.3% each year in the period after the adoption of the currency board. Nevertheless, in 2007 Bulgaria's productivity remained only 36 percent of the EU 27 average.

Even more strikingly, labour productivity in Bulgaria is the lowest in Europe, lower even than Turkey and Romania.

Figure 6. 3 Labour productivity per person employed GDP in Purchasing Power Standards (PPS) per person employed relative to EU-27 (EU-27 = 100)

	1997	**1998**	**1999**	**2000**	**2001**	**2002**	**2003**	**2004**	**2005**	**2006**	**2007**	**2008**
Luxembourg	166.3	165.4	175.9	175.9	162.4	163.3	166.6	169.7	175.7	184	184.4 (f)	181.1 (f)
Ireland	125.4	125.3	125.1	127.1	128	133.3	135.3	134.7	133.9	134.8	135.6 (f)	134.7 (f)
Belgium	137.4	134.4	134.1	136.9	133.8	136.4	134.6	132.1 (b)	132	131.3	131.8 (f)	129.5 (f)
France	125.7	126.3	125.1	125.1	125	125.5	121.6	120.7 (b)	123.2	123.4	123.3 (f)	121.2 (f)
Austria	121.7	122.4	121.8	123	118	119	120.2	120.6	120.4	120.1	120.6 (f)	119.4 (f)
Greece	104.6 (e)	102.0 (e)	102.3 (e)	105.2 (e)	109.9 (e)	114.7 (e)	114.8 (e)	113.7 (e)	116.4 (e)	117.9 (f)	119.8 (f)	119.2 (f)
Finland	110.9	114.1	113.3	114.8	112.7	111.5	109.4	112.7	110.8	112.3	114.1 (f)	113.8 (f)
Sweden	113.2	111.9	113.3	113.5	107.6	107.7	110.1	113.5	113	113.8	114.3 (f)	113.4 (f)
Netherlands	110.2	110.8	111.6	114.4	113.3	113.2	110.9	112.3	114.3	113.2	113.7 (f)	111.6 (f)
EU (15 countries)	114.9	114.6	113.8	113.2	112.5	111.9	111.4	111	110.7	110.4	110.4 (f)	110.1 (f)
United Kingdom	107.1	107.3	107	108.8	109.7	110.1	110.5	112.2	109.7	109.5	111.3 (f)	110.1 (f)
Euro area	117.4	117.1	116	114.7	113.3	112.4	111.8	110.7	110.9	110.5	110.0 (f)	109.5 (f)
Italy	128.8	130	127.4	126	125.5	117.7	115.6	112.1	111	109.1	109.2 (f)	106.8 (f)
Denmark	109.6	108.8	108.2	110.3	107.4	108.4	106.4	108.7	109.3	108.4	107.2 (f)	105.4 (f)
Germany	114.1	112.4	111.8	108	106.8	106.4	108.7	108.3	107.5	107	106.9 (f)	105.3 (f)
EU (27 countries)	100	100	100	100	100	100	100	100	100	100	100.0 (f)	100.0 (f)
Spain	108.3	107.7	105.5	103.7	103.2	104.8	103.8	102.2	102	103	102.7 (f)	99.7 (f)
Malta	:	:	:	96.7	89.9	92	90.3	89.8	90	90.2	90.9 (f)	89.7 (f)
Slovenia	71.8 (e)	73.7 (e)	75.1	75.1	75.4	76.6	78	80.9	82.7	83.9	86.3 (f)	86.9 (f)
Cyprus	80.6 (e)	82.2 (e)	83	85	86.7	84.5	82.6	82.9	84.3	84.8	86.0 (f)	85.6 (f)
Slovakia	54.4 (e)	56.2 (e)	56.5	58	60.4	62.5	63.3	65.5	68.8	71.7	75.8 (f)	77.7 (f)
Hungary	61.5 (e)	62.5 (e)	61.8	64.7	68	70.9	71.8	72.2	73.5	74.4	75.5 (f)	75.1 (f)
Czech Republic	60.5 (e)	60.1 (e)	61.9	61.8	63.3	63	66.6	68.1	69.1	70.7	72.9 (f)	73.3 (f)
Estonia	39.8 (e)	41.2 (e)	43.1	46.5	47.8	50.8	54.5	56.8	61.7	64.2	67.9 (f)	70.0 (f)
Portugal	68.1	67.8	69.2	68.9	68	67.9	68.4	67.1	68.6	68.2 (f)	68.6 (f)	67.6 (f)
Croatia	52.2 (e)	54.4 (e)	54.7 (e)	53.0 (e)	57.8 (e)	58.0 (e)	60.1 (e)	60.9	62.0 (f)	64.2 (f)	65.7 (f)	66.7 (f)
Lithuania	38.0 (e)	40.6 (e)	40.1	42.7	46.9	47.9	51.9	53.3	54.7	57.1	60.1 (f)	62.6 (f)
Poland	49.5 (e)	50.6 (e)	53.9 (e)	55.2 (e)	56.0 (e)	58.6 (e)	60.0 (e)	61.5 (e)	60.9 (e)	60.9 (e)	61.5 (f)	62.1 (f)
Latvia	35.5 (e)	36.8 (e)	37.9	40.1	41.3	43	44.2	45.9	49.2	51.3	55.1 (f)	56.9 (f)
Turkey	40.0 (e)	39.5 (e)	36.2	39.8 (f)	36.4 (f)	38.8 (f)	39.3 (f)	41.5 (f)	42.1 (f)	45.4 (f)	46.6 (f)	47.2 (f)
Romania	:	:	:	:	24.9	29.2	31.1	34.4	36.3	39.2 (f)	40.6 (f)	41.4 (f)
Bulgaria	29.2 (e)	29.9 (e)	30.7	30.4	31.4	33	33.4	33.7	34.3	35	36.0 (f)	36.6 (f)

(:) Not available; (f) Forecast; (b) Break in series; (e) Estimated value
Source: EUROSTAT

A report from the Bulgarian National Bank considers the competitiveness of the manufacturing sector, which by 2002 had become about 95 percent private. Annual productivity gains in manufacturing averaged 8.2 percent, reflecting growth in gross added value against shrinking employment. Productivity performance outweighed wage growth by about six percentage points resulting in a 25 percent cumulative competitive gain in terms of unit labour costs (ULC) between 1997 and 2002.[60] The most successful sub-sectors of the Bulgarian manufacturing industry have been textiles and clothing. Between 1997 and 2002, they gained about 40 percent in ULC competitiveness. Accordingly, their weight in Bulgaria's overall exports grew from 12 to 24 percent (from 23 to 31 percent in EU trade). Its export-import ratio improved, and its share in EU imports from CEEC expanded from 6.4 percent in 1997 to 8.2 percent in 2001. However, more than by increases in productivity, this development has been driven by a significant drop in wages[61] as well as by the role played by foreign capital in the distribution of manufactured goods abroad.

Even more relevant is the importance of Foreign Direct Investment (FDI) in the success of the Bulgarian footwear industry where the share of Bulgarian manufacturers in overall EU imports grew to 7.3 percent. Indeed, in this sector, labour costs increased, productivity decreased and the competitive advantages stemmed only from superior quality and design, along with branding and marketing strategies that come with FDI.

On the other hand, the competitive performance of traditional Bulgarian sectors, such as metals, where foreign industry has not invested, is deteriorating. Bulgarian metallurgy managed at least until 2001 to preserve its share in EU imports from the CEECs. It still maintains a competitive edge in terms of the export-import ratio. But this advantage was seriously eroded during the currency board period, especially with regard to ferrous metals. The overall decline in the export-import ratio is attributed by the Bulgarian National Bank to losses in the cost competitiveness of the sector.

Productivity there declined by 10 percent, while wages grew in real terms by 3 percent between 1997 and 2002.

In conclusion, the traditional manufacturing sector is threatened by a swift participation in EMU insofar as it is not ready yet to compete with foreign capital. The emerging pattern of competitive advantage and export

---

60 Pashev, K., (2003), Competitiveness of the Bulgarian Economy, Bulgarian National Bank, Discussion Papers August 2003

61 Pashev, K., (2003), Competitiveness of the Bulgarian Economy, Bulgarian National Bank, Discussion Papers August 2003

specialisation puts cost competitiveness at the centre of the Bulgarian political economy at least in the short run. In this context, structural reforms prior to participation in EMU, as advocated by the national industry, will constitute the main issues on the policy agenda of competitiveness.

However, this strategy is not necessarily going to win in the medium and long run, when productivity gains through research and innovation will be required.[62]

Conclusion

The evidence confirms the hypotheses drawn from the theoretical framework adopted. Rapid Bulgarian participation in EMU is strongly supported by the domestic financial and banking community, whereas the national industry and its workers seem to have a much more sceptical view of the common currency and its impact on Bulgarian economy.

The explanation for a similar position of the Bulgarian socio-economic sectors vis-à-vis early participation in EMU has been related to the two interrelated dimensions of the level of exchange rates and the exchange rate regime, including in particular the elimination of the devaluation option which entry into EMU would entail. Indeed, as the experience of the currency board already suggests, the adoption of the euro will be accompanied by an appreciation of the Bulgarian exchange rate which, given the level of Bulgarian inflation and the inability to devalue, will reduce the competitiveness of domestic industry. This could lead to the dismantling of the traditional national manufacturing sector and its replacement by more competitive multinational corporations.

References

Andrews, D.M., (1993), "The global origins of the Maastricht Treaty on EMU: closing the window of opportunity", in Cafruny, A. and Rosenthal G.G., (1993), *The state of the European Community: the Maastricht debate and beyond, Longman: Lynne Rienner Publishers.*

62 For a much more detailed analysis of the competitiveness of the Bulgarian manufacturing sector see Pashev, K., (2003), Competitiveness of the Bulgarian Economy, Bulgarian National Bank, Discussion Papers August 2003

—. (1994), “Capital mobility and state autonomy: toward a structural theory of international monetary relations”, in *International Studies Quarterly*, N. 38, p.193-218

Bank for International Settlement (BIS), (1990), *Sixtieth Annual report*, Basle: BIS

Baroncelli, S., Spagnolo, C., and Talani, L.S. (ed) (2008) *Back to Maastricht*, CSP

Bulmer , S., (1983), "Domestic politics and European Community policy-making", in *Journal of Common Market Studies*, Vol. XXI, No. 4, June 1983, p. 354.

Center for Economic Development, (2003), *EU Enlargement and its Impact on the Social Policy and Labour Markets of Accession and Non-Accession Countries Bulgaria Country report*, Sofia 2003

Frieden, J., (1991), "Invested interests: the politics of national economic policies in a world of global finance", in *International Organization*, N. 45, Autumn 199

—. (1994), *The impact of goods and capital market integration on European monetary politics*, Preliminary version, August 1994

Gandolfo, G., (1989), *Corso di economia internazionale*, UTET LIBRERIA

Haas, E.B., (1958), *The uniting of Europe: political, social and economic forces*, Stanford, California: Stanford University Press

Hix, S., (1994), “The study of the European Community: the challenge to comparative politics”, *West European Politics* 17(1): 1-30

Milner, H., (1992), “Theories of cooperation”, in *World Politics*, Vol. 44, pp. 427-495.

—. (1993), “The assumption of anarchy in IR theory: a critique” in Baldwin, D.A., (1993), *Neo-realism and neo-liberalism: the contemporary debate*, Columbia University Press

Moravcsik, A., (1991), "Negotiating the Single European Act: national interests and conventional statecraft in the European Community", in *International Organization*, Vol. 45, No.1, Winter 1991

—. (1993)a, "Preferences and power in the EC: a liberal intergovernmentalist approach", *Journal of Common Market Studies*, vol. 31, No. 4, December 1993, p. 474

—. (1993)b, "Integrating international and domestic theories of international bargaining" in Evans, P.B., Jacobson, H.K., Putnam, R.D., (1993), *Double-edged diplomacy: international bargaining and domestic policy*, Berkeley: University of California Press

Padoa-Schioppa, T., (1988), "The European monetary system: a long term view", in Giavazzi, F., Micossi, S. and Miller, M., (1988), *The European Monetary System*, Cambridge: Cambridge University Press

Pashev, K., (2003), *Competitiveness of the Bulgarian Economy*, Bulgarian National Bank, Discussion Papers August 2003

Putnam, R., (1988), "Diplomacy and domestic politics", in *International Organization*, Vol. 42

Rosamond, B., (1995), "Mapping the European condition: the theory of integration and the integration of theory", *European Journal of International Relations*, , Vol. 1 (3): 391-408

Sandholtz, W., (1993), "Choosing Union: monetary politics and Maastricht" in *International Organization*, Vol. 47, pp. 1-39

Talani, L.S., (2004), European Political Economy, Political Science perspectives, London: Ashgate

Tsoukalis, L., (1997), *The Political Economy of the European Union*, Oxford University Press

References in Bulgarian

Чобанов, Д. Приемането на Еврото в България, ИПИ,

Chobanov, D., Adopting the Euro in Bulgaria, IME (http://www.ime-bg.org/pdf_docs/papers/Euro_Adoption_D.pdf)

Чобанов, Д. Бордът е най-подходящият паричен режим до приемането на еврото, ИПИ, Преглед на стопанската политика, бр. 347/ 12.10.2007

Chobanov, D., The Currency Board is the Most Appropriate Monetary Regime until Adopting the Euro, Economic Policy Review No. 347/ 12 Oct. 2007, IME, Sofia (http://ime.bg/bg/articles/bordyt-e-naj-podhodqshtiqt-parichen-revim-do-priemaneto-na-ewroto/)

Еврозоната – пореден тест за България и Румъния, в. Дневник, 3.10.2006

Eurozone – Another Test for Bulgaria and Romania, Dnevnik Daily, 3.10.2006 (http://evropa.dnevnik.bg/show/?storyid=285286)

Въвеждането на еврото в България е реалистично да стане в рамките на следващите пет години, БНР, 18.09.2007

Introducing the Euro in Bulgaria is Feasible within the Next Five Years, BNR, 18.09.2007 http://www.bnr.bg/radiobulgaria/emission_bulgarian/news/1809-6.htm

Европа-Инфо, Инфо Радио, 14.07.2006

Europe-Info, Info Radio, 14.07.2006

http://www.inforadio.bg/euroinfo.php?item=484

Ангелов, Г., Еврозоната – една цел, различни подходи, Политики, бр. 04/07, Институт "Отворено общество" София

Angelov, G., Eurozone – One Target, Various Approaches, Policies, Issue 04/07, Open Society Institute, Sofia
http://politiki.bg/?cy=72&lang=1&a0i=222905&a0m=readInternal&a0p_id=223

България и балтийските страни влизат в еврозоната през 2010-2011 г.

Bulgaria and the Baltic States to Enter the Eurozone in 2010-2011
http://www.expert.bg/?act=news&id=94559

България бърза да приеме Еврото, в. Сега, 28.03.2007

Bulgaria Hurries to Adopt the Euro, Sega Daily, 28.03.2007

България може да приеме Еврото през 2010 г., според анализ на UniCredit, Expert.bg Business News, 11.10.2007,

Bulgaria May Adopt the Euro in 2010, UniCredit Analysts Say, Expert.bg Business News, 11.10.2007
http://analysis.expert.bg/?analysis_id=325

Еврото, 23.03.2007, Финанси БГ

The EURO, Finance BG, 23.03.2007
http://financebg.com/?act=showarticles&more=14062

България трябва да избере внимателно момента на влизането си в Еврозоната и да информира широко гражданите за промяната, 18.07.2006, Икономически и социален съвет

Bulgaria Must Carefully Choose the Moment of its Accession to the Eurozone and Broadly Inform the Public about the Change, 18.07.2006, Economic and Social Council
http://www.esc.bg/newsfullview.php?lang=0&id=105

УниКредит: Словакия ще е първата, която ще последва Словения в Еврозоната, 28.02.2007, Investor.bg

UniCredit: Slovakia will be the First to Follow Slovenia in the Eurozone, 28.02.2007, Investor.bg
http://www.investor.bg/?cat=91&id=47443

Николов, И., Източното разширяване на Еврозоната. Новите ползи и старите шокове, в. Капитал, бр. 29, 21 юли 2006

Nikolov, I., The Eastern Enlargement of the Eurozone. New Benefits and Old Shocks, Capital Weekly, Issue 29/ 21.07.2006
http://www.capital.bg/show.php?storyid=273328

Аврамов, Р., Когато властта е мекушава, шансовете за приемане на Еврото намаляват, в. Капитал, бр. 26, 29 юни 2007

Avramov, R., When the Government is Hesitant and Meek, Chances for Adopting the Euro Decrease, Capital Weekly, Issue 26/ 29.06.2007 http://www.capital.bg/show.php?storyid=354200

Сигнал от ЕЦБ: Засега забравете за еврото и намалете темпото, в. Дневник, 10.10.2007

Signal from ECB: Forget about the Euro at Present and Slow Down the Pace, Dnevnik Daily, 10.10.2007 http://www.dnevnik.bg/show/print.php?storyid=385338

Йорданов, Б., "Банк Аустрия кредитанщалт: България може да приеме еврото около 2010 г.", в. Дневник, 18.08.2005

Yordanov, B., "Bank Austria Creditanstalt: Bulgaria May Adopt the Euro around 2010", Dnevnik Daily, 18.08.2005 http://evropa.dnevnik.bg/show/print.php?storyid=198755

Трудният път към Еврото, в. Капитал, бр. 15, 13 април 2007

The Difficult Way to the Euro, Capital Weekly, Issue 15/ 13.04.2007 http://www.capital.bg/show.php?storyid=330539

ЕЦБ: България може да влезе в ЕВМ 2 не по-рано от есента, 8.06.2007

ECB: Bulgaria May Enter the ERM II Not Earlier than in the Autumn, 8.06.2007 http://money.ibox.bg/news/id_740900588

Орешарски: Влизането ни в ЕВМ 2 може да породи негативи, 1.06.2007

Oresharski: Our Entry in ERM II May Have Negative Effects, 1.06.2007 http://money.ibox.bg/news/id_513357807

Искров: Валутният борд ще улесни приемането на еврото, 27.04.2007

Iskrov: The Currency Board Will Facilitate the Adoption of the Euro, 27.04.2007 http://money.ibox.bg/news/id_970705568

БНБ: Ще се преборим с инфлационния критерий за приемане на еврото, 31.05.2007,

BNB: We Shall Cope with the Inflation Criteria for Adopting the Euro, 31.05.2007 http://money.ibox.bg/news/id_316004288

България отлага с две години въвеждането на еврото, 1.02.2007,

Bulgaria Postpones with Two Years the Adoption of the Euro, 1.02.2007 http://money.ibox.bg/news/id_734741691

България може да въведе еврото преди други страни от Централна Европа, 11.05.2006

Bulgaria May Adopt the Euro before Other Central European Countries, 11.05.2006 http://www.mediapool.bg/show/?storyid=117159

Приемането на еврото в България, ИПИ, Преглед на стопанската политика, 25.07.2007

The Adoption of the Euro in Bulgaria, IME, Economic Policy Review, 25.07.2007 http://ime-bg.org/pr_bg/177-5.htm

Европейски акценти, РФИ, 22.03.2007

European Highlights, Radio France International – Bulgaria, 22.03.2007 http://www.rfi.bg/prog/euaccent/show.shtml?type=show&program=euaccent&news_NUM=915&indcxa=no

Simeonov, K., Public Opinion in Bulgaria on the Road towards the Eurozone, Alternativi Journal, UNWE, http://alternativi.unwe.acad.bg/br14/05_-_Kaloyan_Simeonov.doc

CONCLUSION

PANACEA OR PUBLIC DEBATE?

SUSAN L. WOODWARD

In the conventional wisdom, European integration and European enlargement are synonymous. The outcome of the progressive enlargement of the European Union to include all the countries on the continent (and in some conceptions, further beyond) is, almost by definition, ever greater integration, and such integration is uniformly a good thing. All benefit.

In the case of south-eastern Europe, where the violent break-up of Yugoslavia revived the late 19th and early 20th century stereotype of "Balkanization" and the region's threat to European security, integration is also the antidote to disintegration. EU membership for states in south-eastern Europe will not only bring economic prosperity, democratic consolidation, and European values of tolerance, multiculturalism, and human rights; even the incentive of membership is enough to cause politicians to cooperate, people to reconcile, and voters to choose alternatives to nationalism. This security gain of EU integration, that the accession process was itself the best route to peace and stability for the region and for Europe as a whole, thus led the EU to impose a third set of requirements for EU membership on the countries of the western Balkans, not an accession process but a stabilization and accession process (SAP).

These high hopes are readily apparent in the two articles on Macedonia in this volume. For Zhidas Daskalovski, the rapid move toward EU accession (signing a stabilization and accession agreement in 2001 and gaining candidate status in 2005) has erased the conditions that led Macedonia to the brink of civil war with Albanian insurgents in February-June 2001 and the threat of further disintegration over the remaining disputes over Macedonian sovereignty and continuing fears among many that the recognition by 41 states as of June 2008 of Albanian rights to self-determination in Kosovo will only encourage Albanians in Macedonia to continue their related struggle. Moreover, the positive effect of the EU (and US) imposed constitutional reform on democratic consolidation, reversing Albanian grievances and lack of identity with and loyalty to the Macedonian state, will also work in Kosovo when the EU administers the judiciary and police, for an indeterminate period, together with a continued presence of NATO troops. Dane Taleski's public opinion surveys show overwhelming support in Macedonia for EU membership (87 to 92 % between 2003 and 2007)), high expectations for its positive effect on economic development (51%), a rise in support when the EU sends a positive signal, and deep dissatisfaction with the pace of accession. This public opinion is also uncritical, both of what EU membership might entail and bring and of the threat coming from the much lower level of support in EU states for another round of enlargement. Disillusionment will not be with the EU but with the Macedonian government and political leaders.

The difficulty with this conventional wisdom, as the other authors show, is its conflict with the facts. The disintegration of Yugoslavia, for example, was a direct result of the high hopes for EU membership in Slovenia in 1988-90 and expectations (justified, it turned out) of a positive EU response which led to its secession and the eventual breakup of Yugoslavia. EU failure at conflict prevention and crisis management is widely seen as a cause of at least two of its wars. Bakalova argues, in fact, that EU integration makes nationalist views and policies more intense in general, not less. Its conditionality on minority rights legitimizes the very nationalist demands that threaten disintegration; its repeated double standards in response to different nationalist projects in the region send deeply mixed messages; and the ongoing debate between supranational and national identities and Euroscepticism questioning the price of integration, both among old and new members, are leading to a reassertion of national identities and national interests. Taleski, too, shows that public opinion in member states on whether to continue EU enlargement varies according to country, that is, that there is no EU supranational identity on what the composition of its members should be. National differences remain.

According to Gordon, there has also been a consistent divergence between the promises of EU norms and rhetoric and its actions on minority rights, with an astonishing disinterest in benchmarks for and actual progress on the protection of human and minority rights in the annual reports on each country in the SAA process, despite its rhetorical demands and declared conditions for membership. The EU accession process as a conflict resolution mechanism has, at all stages for south-eastern Europe, also been inappropriate to the needs of post-conflict countries, despite the explicit design of both Royaumont and the stabilization and accession formula to use the process and regional integration to address these needs. Its top-down approach, trickle-down expectations, and extremely meager funds for projects addressed to this goal all reinforce her argument on minority rights, that the EU does not follow-through operationally on the non-economic aspects of integration.

The economic aspects of EU enlargement, too, however, will necessarily create losers as well as winners, Talani shows. In the Bulgarian case, even membership does not prevent this differentiation. Domestic manufacturers, workers, and consumers all expect to be losers when Bulgaria joins the EMU, while domestic financial and banking sectors and multinational manufacturing companies expect to be winners.

This paradox of expectations and reality has an explanation, Ralchev argues. Government policies to adopt the accession requirements in each country reflect elite interests in membership, but because these policies include many that would be deeply unpopular and possibly destabilizing, there is a second stage of adoption in which elites make a concerted effort to mobilize the media, civil society organizations, and political parties around a discourse to justify the policies and prevent a critical discourse.

If, as this conventional wisdom increasingly holds, the fate of democracy itself in south-eastern Europe depends on EU membership, then it would seem vital to have a democratic debate on the conventional wisdom as well. As Taleski writes, what will happen if the government achieves progress in EU integration, but the economic and social progress Macedonians expect does not occur? What will be the effect on Macedonian democracy? Talani's data suggest that the political consequences in Bulgaria also will not be as smooth as the unexamined consensus suggests.

Surely a safer path would be a democratization of the EU process rather than the top-down, imposed, and manipulated method described in these chapters. A more open, informed debate might conclude in each country in the region that the benefits of EU membership outweigh the costs, but then national policies could be taken to address those costs and attempt to manage their potential threats to political stability and regional security in the course of the transition. Yet without public pressure from democratic debate, Taleski argues, governments in the region will have no reason to contemplate and design such policies even if they would benefit all.

The lack of challenge and debate on the costs and benefits of EU membership, these authors imply, has also hindered empirical research on the question. Yet without such research, appropriate adjustment policies are impossible. They have identified three issues on which to begin: the security consequences of EU approaches to nationalism and civil war, the democratic consequences of EU approaches to minority rights, and the economic consequences of monetary and financial integration. These are only a start in a vital direction, but the range of data these authors use already – EU progress reports on specific countries, monies actually allocated and disbursed in PHARE, EIDHR, and CARDS, public opinion polls, interviews with representatives of unions and employers, across sectors, and textual analysis of normative and operational documents – demonstrate much room for further research. These articles suggest that the immediate effect of the way the EU is managing the process of accession in south-eastern Europe is to reduce the very political consensus that is presumed necessary to commitment during the protracted and costly process.